Permit Me Voyage

Permit Me Voyage

"Permit me voyage, Love, into your Hands."
Hart Crane and James Agee

Sermons By

R. Maurice Boyd

B.A., Lic. Mus., D.D.

Minister of The Fifth Avenue Presbyterian Church
New York

WELCH PUBLISHING COMPANY INC.
Burlington, Ontario, Canada

ISBN: 1-55011-012-8
© 1989 by R. Maurice Boyd

WELCH PUBLISHING COMPANY INC.
960 The Gateway
Burlington, ON
L7L 5K7 Canada

Printed in Canada

To

Leslie, Heather and Jennifer
With Love.

CONTENTS

Introduction: For Preachers Only   9

1. Ways of Loving 11

2. How to Forgive Yourself 24

3. Remembering to Forget 35

4. The Attractiveness of Failure 44

5. Born Again? 53

6. The Judgment of Judging 66

7. Come Out the Wilderness! 76

8. Death in the Desert 88

9. Permit Me Voyage 98

10. How to be Indignant 110

11. The Temptation to be Christian 122

12. True Simplicity 130

13. The Moving Finger 140

14. What Easter Gives Back to Us 149

For Preachers Only

When a great poet is so deeply influenced by a great preacher that he writes a poem about it, preachers ought to read it.

When W. H. Auden wrote *At the Grave of Henry Irving*, he acknowledged that its insight and inspiration were derived from his friend Reinhold Niebuhr. The two used to discuss the hazards of their respective callings. Each taught and learned from the other the vanity and treason of their work. That is why the poem is a cry for help, an appeal for intercession for both of them and for all preachers, God help us!

> All will be judged. Master of nuance and scruple,
> Pray for me and for all writers living or dead,
> Because there are many whose works
> Are in better taste than their lives; because there is no end
> To the vanity of our calling: make intercession
> For the treason of all clerks.

I know the truth of this because I know one preacher very well and many preachers quite well.

But it's not only preachers who are aware of this vanity and treason. Indeed, some preachers are not aware of it at all. But our people are, and always have been. Not only Auden, and Hardy, and MacDonald, and Lewis, and Huxley, who have poems to prove it, but all the perceptive ones who hear us. They know our temptation to conceit, the pretension, the inordinate self-regard, and how easily we claim for ourselves the qualities that properly belong only to our message. They know how easily we are seduced into believing that we are as good as we sound.

What *we* need to believe, of course, is that preachers, too,

9

live by the Grace and Mercy of Him who is the Author and
Giver of all good things.

Now the wonder of the Gospel is that there is grace even for
professional holy men like us who are so used to handling the
outsides of holy things. And this grace is not only *for* us, but
through us, making us means of grace to others. If there is no
end to the vanity of our calling, there is no end, either, to God's
infinite pity.

And for those of you who decided to cheat a little and, not
being preachers, read what was written for preachers only, there
is for you, too, the same saving mercy. We are quite sure of this,
for we know that if God can do something with preachers, then
no one is beyond His reach.

And so a prayer:

> From all my lame defeats and oh! much more
> From all the victories that I seemed to score;
> From cleverness shot forth on Thy behalf
> At which, while angels weep, the audience laugh;
> Thou, who wouldst give no sign, deliver me . . .
> Lord of the narrow gate and the needle's eye,
> Take from me all my trumpery lest I die.

[C. S. Lewis *The Apologist's Evening Prayer*]

R. Maurice Boyd
New York,
September, 1989

WAYS OF LOVING

1 Corinthians 13

The highest expression of the Christian religion is to love God with heart and soul and mind and strength, and our neighbour as ourselves. The two greatest commandments say so, and in them all the other commandments are fulfilled.

To love is the highest expression of Christian faith because when we love we share the divine nature. Clement of Alexandria used to say that every real Christian practices being God. We practice being God by loving as He loves, and in this way become partakers of the divine nature. It is interesting to note that in the New Testament the highest test of genuine faith is not orthodoxy — not believing the right things or holding the correct opinions — but loving with the love of Christ. Those who love know God, but the unloving know nothing of God, for God *is* love.

Yet we are all aware that the word "love" is used to express so many feelings of the heart, so many convictions of the mind, and so many actions of the body, that its meaning is blurred. We hardly know what we are talking about when we speak of it. How are we to understand the meaning of love? Let me make four exhortations in the hope of distinguishing things that differ, and of making its meaning clear.

I.   *Let your affection be considerate.*

Reinhold Niebuhr once warned that we Christians are never more dangerous than when we act from love, because love can lull the conscience to sleep and our affection can conceal from us our insensitivity and unkindness. Niebuhr was right. We can see this in all our relationships and especially in

11

those characterized by affection. It is often plain, for example, in the relationship of parents and children.

I know a mother who uses her affection for her children as a means to control them. Even though they are now grown up, she thinks she has the right to pry into their private affairs and to know everything about where they go, what they do, and whom they meet. The only way her children can discourage her is by having an unhappy confrontation with her. And when they do, she becomes upset, complaining that they are unkind and ungrateful, and that they have deeply wounded one who does what she does only because she loves them. As a result, her children are left feeling guilty and resentful, and the mother has confirmed her control of them. She goes on asking questions that are none of her business. She has affection but she has no considerateness.

Now, there was a time when her attitude was perfectly appropriate. When our children are small we must do most of their thinking for them. If we don't, they may be drowned, or burned to death, or run over by motor cars. We must be vigilant for them, guarding them from dangers they do not recognize.

As they grow up, however, wisdom tells us to draw back a little. We encourage them to think their own thoughts, to express them in their own way, to form their own opinions, to make their own decisions. There is a view of creation that sees it not as God's action, but as God's restraint; Our courteous God draws back a little to give His creatures room to be and to grow. That ought to be the pattern of our relationship with our children. Surely there comes a time when we stand a handbreadth off to give our children room to grow. Or, to put it another way, our affection should be considerate.

When this does not happen, the result is often great unhappiness. Then, as we say, mother love becomes "smother" love. But it is not only mothers who are guilty of it; fathers are guilty of it as well. We have all met a mother's boy or a "daddy's little girl" who have remained emotionally dependent on their parents even though grown to manhood or womanhood, and who consequently have been unable to establish or sustain healthy and satisfying relationships with members of the opposite sex. I know a man in his forties who still asks his father's permission before planning to attend any event, however innocent. Otherwise he would offend the affection his father has for him. But it is an affection that has little consideration for the no-longer-young man, for it perpetuates his sense of dependence, and is therefore selfish and manipulative.

Sometimes this lack of consideration has less serious but still unhappy consequences. C. S. Lewis tells of having lunch with a minister and his wife and their two children, a young man and a young woman home from university for the weekend. The young people were thoughtful, intelligent, perceptive. But at the dinner table their father dominated every conversation, whatever the subject, and treated the opinions of his children with impatience. He hardly listened to them. When they expressed their point of view, he immediately made little of it until at last they grew silent. They did not argue with their father because their mother had already made it clear that arguments upset her. So the young people sat there, humiliated and seething with resentment until their first opportunity to decently make an escape. Because the affection of the parents for their children lacked considerateness, the young people were diminished; and because of the affection of the children for their parents, they did not confront their father as they would any other arrogant know-all. They couldn't risk upsetting him, or their mother. How could they, knowing that their parents loved them so much!

We sometimes say that because home is a place of genuine affection, we can be ourselves there and speak our minds freely, knowing that we shall be understood, or at least accepted. But when affection is lacking in respect, this does not happen. For many, home becomes the one place where they do not feel free to say what they think. Their opinions receive less hospitality at home than anywhere else.

Let me suggest a good test for the considerateness of our affection. Do we treat our own children with the same respect we show their friends when they come to visit? When their friends are our guests we listen to them with care and are thoughtful in our response. When our own children talk to us we often listen with only half our attention and our response is often careless and lazy. We take them for granted, our affection makes us presumptuous, and we act as though our love excused our discourtesy.

Affection that is not considerate produces a further sadness. It may mean that we lose the joy of a relationship with our children based on mutual respect, a wholesome reticence, and the recognition of them as independent beings with their own right to privacy.

One of the great joys of my life is to discover that sometimes my children's insights are sharper and wiser than my own. At times my children are more perceptive and more sensitive than I am. I can ask their advice and get good advice, often better than anything I could have thought of myself. And they know me better than I know myself. To have their friendship is better than to have an echo. Why should we ever wish for a subservient, totally predictable child when we might have an independent, creative and wise person with whom to enjoy a mutually enriching relationship? But such a rewarding relationship is not possible if we use our affection to manipulate and possess our children. We must not attempt to keep them ours by making them feel guilty when they wish to put a little distance between themselves and us.

Some parents distort the relationship by reminding their youngsters of how much they have done for them and how much they have sacrificed on their behalf. This is not only unfair but untrue. If we made sacrifices for our children it was because we wanted to; it was our own choice. It was for ourselves that we did it, as well as for them, and to use what we did to lay a burden of obligation and guilt on them is dishonest. If they owe anybody anything, it is not really to us that they owe it. They did not ask to be born, and they certainly did not ask to be born into our family. If they have an indebtedness to pay, then surely the obligation is to their own children. Perhaps the best way they can acknowledge the care we showed to them is to treat their own children with the same care. But we must not

make them feel a lifelong obligation to us, a burden of indebtedness which they cannot discharge or escape. If we do, they
will resent it.

The love we have for our children doesn't give us the right
to control them and pry into their lives and know everything
about them. They do not want that. We should not want that.
But an affection shaped and refined by considerateness makes
possible a relationship of mutual appreciation and delight.

II.   *Let your friendship be disinterested.*

Malcolm Muggeridge observes that the most enjoyable
aspect of friendship is that it is the most disinterested of
human relationships. It is as disinterested as a human relationship can be.

By disinterested, we do not mean that we should not be
interested in our friends, nor do we mean that we should not
care for them. Friendship is disinterested because we are not
in it for anything other than itself. We are not in it for power,
or influence, or prestige, or anything that it might offer us, but
just for the thing itself.

Yet, in a sense, we are not in it even for friendship. Have
you noticed that people who are desperate for friendship have
very few friends? The reason for this is no mystery. We do not
find friends by looking for them; we have friends when we discover that there are others who are interested in the same
things we are interested in, who share the same concerns and
hold the same matters to be important. We form friendships
not by seeking them, but by discovering that others are as
interested in music, or literature, or religion, or baseball, as we
are. Good friends do not always agree when questions are discussed, but they do agree about the questions worth discussing. C. S. Lewis tells us that we think of lovers face to face,
looking at each other, absorbed in each other. My friends and
I hardly ever look at each other; we are too busy looking out to
sea, or at a stream where the trout are rising, or in a book, or at
an opera.

Let me put it another way. One of the most satisfying things about the disinterestedness of friendship is that it is not jealous or possessive. The love of lovers often is. We know that sexual love is for two only, and that the nature of it is changed if a third person is permitted to intrude. But we do not say that about friendship. Friends set no limit on the number who can share their friendship so long as the basic requirements of integrity, consideration and trust are met. And their openness is for a very good reason. Added friends bring added richness to all. A new friend reveals things in my old friends that I hadn't noticed and brings parts of me alive for others that they could not bring alive for themselves. The richness of friendship is multiplied, for each friend discovers others in a unique way to the benefit of all.

Not long ago I spent a few days with a group of male friends. What a varied lot we were! It was our love of boats and the sea and fishing that brought us together. Money, fame, power, education, reputation mattered not at all; what did matter was a mutual care and a deeply shared interest. Each person brought to the group not only the distinctiveness of his own personality, but the qualities he drew out of the others. One of the most joyous things about friendship is that we bring each other alive for our friends. The sad thing is there is so little of such friendship around.

Read about "The Inklings," a group of men who used to meet in a pub at Oxford. It was named "The Eagle and Child" but they called it "The Bird and Baby." They went to the pub and drank beer and smoked pipes and read and talked. C. S. Lewis first read *The Screwtape Letters* there. Tolkien first read *The Hobbit* there. Charles Williams attended, and many others who had a love for literature and the frank exchange of opinions and the testing of new ideas. Oh, to have been a fly on the wall of "The Bird and Baby" while that was going on! I should think the group continues to meet regularly in heaven where most of them are now.

Or think of *God's Apology*, a book written to celebrate the lifelong friendship of three men, Hesketh Pearson, Hugh Kingsmill and Malcolm Muggeridge. The title is from a saying

of Hugh Kingsmill that "friends are God's apology for relations." And what a friendship theirs was, centered in their
enduring love of life and literature, their contempt for all who
sought power, and their mockery of all human pretensions. It
enlivened every part of their life, and enriched our society for
years.

About our dear friends, our kindred spirits, we feel as
Gorky felt about Tolstoy. Seeing him once sitting on a rock by
the seashore with his chin on his hand and his elbow on his
knee, Gorky said, "As long as that man lives I will not be an
orphan in this world."

That is friendship, and it must be disinterested. It is not
that friends do not help each other; they do, but they are not
there to be used. They are not *for* anything. They are valued for
themselves. They are our friends.

III.   *Let your passion be splendid.*

This does not mean, of course, that our passion should
always be like *Tristan and Isolde*. Who could stand or sustain
such intensity? Our sense of humour will not allow us to make
our passionate love as desperate and all-consuming as that. It
does mean that our passion should be splendid in its nobility,
in its appreciation and cherishing of the beloved, in its generosity. Christians should know a great deal about this. I have
always believed that Christians ought to make the very best
lovers, for their love-making has a dimension to it that unbelievers do not have and cannot enjoy.

In every wedding I perform I declare that marriage "was
ordained by God that instincts and affections *given by Him*
might be fulfilled and perfected in purity and holiness." Given
by Him! Making love is God's loving intention, His gracious
gift to us, part of that world which He created and pronounced
good. Christians ought to make the very best lovers, for in
making love they celebrate a good gift of God. Yet often it is
far from the splendid, joyous thing God meant it to be. It is
often the occasion, not of great joy, but of great fear and guilt.

Often it is not splendid, but reluctant, bestowed hesitantly or grudgingly, something that is necessary but not something to be enjoyed, required for the continuation of the species but not anything for which we ought to be thankful or to be celebrated with delight. Some Christians feel that it may be all right to make love so long as they don't enjoy it. But if we are not to enjoy it, why did God make it so enjoyable?

Let me tell you when passion is splendid. It is splendid, not when we have sex, but when we make love. When we have sex we are fulfilling an animal function. Birds and bees and all orders of creation do it. There is nothing distinctively human about it. When we have sex, often what we are looking for is a sensation in our own body for which it is necessary to use another body. As Lewis somewhere remarks, the man who is merely lustful says that what he wants is a woman, but in fact that is the last thing he wants. He does not want a woman, he wants an experience for which a woman's body is necessary. There is nothing splendid in that. It may be nothing higher than two people using each other. Indeed, it is sometimes merely selfish or even commercial. There is little caring in it. That is why someone remarked cynically that when a young man says to a young woman, "I love you," what he really means is, "I love me and I want you!"

But when we make love we do not want a woman, we want *this* woman; and we want not only her body, but all of her — all the wonder and mystery of her to marvel at and adore. We want her mind and her spirit, her sensitivity and her kindness, her trust and her fears. We want to be responsible for her, to take her to our heart and life forever. When we make love we receive another person to ourselves, and give ourselves in return. Then our passion is splendid.

Having sex is often an isolated experience, not only in the sense that it may happen only once, but in the deeper sense that it may be separated from all that properly leads to and flows from making love. Making love is never an isolated event. It derives its splendor from all that goes before it and what follows after it. We can no more isolate it than we can separate one wave of the sea from those waves that run ahead and those that pursue. Do you know what we call those other waves? We call them respect, and cherishing, and tenderness, and adoration. Do you know what it means to cherish? It is the loveliest word in the marriage-service and one of the loveliest in our language. It means "to hold in one's heart." That is making love. That is God's good gift to us. And it may be splendid.

Nathaniel Hawthorne once wrote to his fiancée, the woman with whom a few years later he set up and perpetuated a radiantly happy Christian home, "You know I love you dearly, but let me tell you that there is that about you that fills my soul with awe, which turns my love into religion." That makes passion splendid.

But there is another thing: Our passion is splendid when it enables us to love more and better. William James used to say that to express an emotion is not only to express it, but to strengthen it. The feeling is deepened in the telling and by the telling. When our passion is splendid, filled with appreciation, cherishing and tenderness, then the act of love-making actually makes love. It increases our capacity to love and adore.

Let me tell you something else. Our passion is splendid when it elevates the person we love. When we know, not only that we are held in affection but desired as lovers, that knowledge sets us among kings and princes. And there is nothing that so diminishes our sense of personal worth and dignity, nothing that so strikes at the root of our self-esteem, than to feel that we are not attractive or desirable to the person we love. Yet husbands and wives are often careless about this; they take each other for granted and settle for comfort without romance.

Something else about our passion must be splendid. We love splendidly when the one we love finds in our love the meaning of their life. Everyone does what they do for somebody; and when there isn't anyone who cares and cherishes and loves, then life loses its zest and all initiative is blunted. Then courage and fortitude are lost and the will to succeed is gone. I know men who look at their appointment-books and ask themselves how they're ever going to get through the coming week. I know women who think of the next few months and don't know how they will manage to cope with all that will be required of them. What a sense of desolation can sweep over us when we consider the demands on our time and energy! Do you know what makes the difference between fulfillment and emptiness? Often it is having someone to love, and to love us, for whom we do all that we do, and who makes all that we do worthwhile. Do you remember what it meant to us as children to have some little success at school and to rush home to share it with someone whose love gave it all the meaning it had? Think of the difference it would have made if there had been no one at home who cared!

I know a woman in Hamilton, Ontario, who went to visit the steel company there and saw for the first time what her husband did for a living as he worked at the great blast furnaces in almost unbearable heat. She broke down and cried. "I never knew you had to do that for a living," she told her husband. "How do you do it?" Of course he knew how and why he did it. He did it because he loved her, and because she loved and cherished him. That was the energy of his life. Everybody needs someone for whom they do what they do.

Do you believe that what I've been saying is true? If it is even half true, why is it that so many men put so much of their energy into their work and so little into their relationship with their wives, that everything they work for is threatened? Why is it that so many women love their children with so much love and devotion that they neglect their husbands, so that their children's security is threatened? Do we not know that the best thing a husband can do for his children is to cherish their mother, and that the best thing a mother can do for her children is to love their father?

Let me ask you another question! If what I have said is true, then why are there so many men who have not heard their wives say "I love you" in the last ten years, and women who never hear words of tenderness and appreciation from their husbands? Why is it that when passion *can* be so splendid and so pervasively enriching, it is often so careless, lazy and mechanical that it diminishes the one relationship that makes our whole life meaningful? Why is it that our passion, far from being the splendid thing it might be, is not even satisfying? Not only does our love-making not make love; it becomes the occasion of estrangement and hostility.

This will have been a useful sermon if it enables those who love each other to talk about their relationship and to tell of their love. If you are neglecting the most intimate part of your relationship, you must not be surprised if everything else begins to crumble and your marriage starts to disintegrate.

Further, our love-making will be splendid if we think of it not as something we take, but as something we give. If we have to take it, the joy will go out of it. The deepest part of us does not want to take but longs to give. If we think of making love as something we give, then we shall discover that when both give, nobody has to take, and both can joyously receive.

IV.   *Let your charity be Christ-like.*

For a Christian, charity must be Christ-like, because the very word for charity, for love, is the Greek word *agape*. It was a neutral word until Christians got hold of it. It was an almost empty word, hardly known in secular Greek until the time of the New Testament. That is why the early Christians chose it. The writers of the New Testament looked for an empty word into which they could pour all they had learned of the love of God in Jesus, and all He had taught of loving one another. They took this empty word and made it their own forever. *Agape* became the word for Christian love, a word which was defined by what they had seen and heard in Him. *Agape* is the love we see in Jesus Christ.

Henry Drummond said once that the Apostle Paul wrote 1 Corinthians 13 with Jesus Christ in mind. It is a description of Christian love, for it is a description of Jesus. To prove it, all you have to do is take out the word love, and put in His name. It fits perfectly. Listen to it:

> Jesus is patient; He is kind and envies no one. He is never boastful, nor conceited, nor rude. He is never selfish. He is not quick

to take offence. Christ keeps no score of wrongs; He does not gloat over other men's sins, but delights in the truth. There is nothing He cannot face; there is no limit to His faith, His love, and His endurance . . .

For the Christian, the very word for charity, for love, means Christ-likeness.

This quality of Christ-likeness refines all our other loves. *Agape* means my concern for your well-being. It means that no other love I have, whether it is affection, or friendship, or passion, can be allowed to harm you in any way. To have *agape* means that my affection will be considerate, my friendship disinterested, my passion splendid. That is what Christian love means, for it seeks only the highest good of the beloved. It means I must never use you as a means to my ends. It is the standard by which the quality of all our other loves is judged, and it is the norm by which we judge our conduct.

And *agape* is an action word. It has to do with what a Christian does; it is directed, not by feelings but by the will. That is why it can be commanded. *Agape* is commandment-love. Affection, friendship and passion are not like that. They have to do with feelings, interests, inclinations. But *agape* asks not how we felt, but how we acted. Samuel Johnson remarked once that "kindness is within our power, affection is not." *Agape* is within our power, for it is an unshakable, Christ-like attitude of goodwill. We can do it. It means seeking our neighbour's highest good, and we can do that whether we like our neighbour or not.

I'm sure you've noticed that when you treat people right you begin to *feel* right about them. *Agape* may begin as an act of will, but it need not end there. Treat others with an unwearied goodwill and you will find that what began as an act of will soon begins to affect your feelings. We may begin by showing *agape* to someone we don't like. We may end by not only loving them, but liking them.

Let me end with a story. Several days after President Kennedy was assassinated, a Presbyterian church in Ann Arbor, Michigan, wrote to Marina Oswald, the wife of Lee Harvey

Oswald who had been charged with the assassination. They had heard that she wanted to stay in America, and that she wanted to learn to speak English. They wrote to her and invited her to come to Ann Arbor and promised to find a home for her. They arranged with the university to teach her English. But when word of what they were doing got out, the mail started pouring in. Most of it was critical of both church and university. Some letters said their actions were unpatriotic, un-American. One woman wrote to say that she had been going to church for forty years and nothing like this had ever happened to her!

The minister, whom I know and admire enormously, answered every letter, paying particular attention to the letters that were critical. He ended every letter he wrote in the same way: "The one thing you have not shown us is that what we have done is unlike Christ."

That is the test, because in the end, being a Christian just means seeing with His eyes, feeling with His heart, judging with His truth and grace, feeling with His compassion, and loving with His love. That is what it means to be a Christian. So let your charity be Christ-like. If you think that is going to make us all the same, then you don't know many saints. The most marvelous thing about them is that they are all so different from one another, and so like Him.

Let your affection be considerate. Let your friendship be disinterested. Let your passion be splendid. And let your charity be Christ-like. That is what He asks. Indeed, He not only asks it but gives us grace to do it.

HOW TO FORGIVE YOURSELF

Peter found it difficult to forgive others. He asked our Lord, "How many times do I forgive my brother when he keeps on wronging me? Seven times?" Our Lord replied, "Not seven times, Peter, but seventy times seven." By that He did not mean 490 times. In our Lord's arithmetic, "seventy times seven" is an infinite number, and because love keeps no score of wrongs there can be no limit to our willingness to forgive. What kind of forgiveness is it that keeps count until a limit is reached which ends all obligations of mercy, and we can then get even? Peter's difficulty was not resolved by our Lord's answer, it was increased. Jesus had made forgiveness of others harder than ever. The disciples saw at once that such forgiveness is not humanly possible, so their question became a prayer, "Lord, increase our faith!" And He did.

Hard as it is to forgive others, many find it even harder to forgive themselves. Is that your experience? Many of us are more gracious and generous to others than we are with ourselves. So this morning I am going to speak of the difficulty of self-forgiveness. If you are a person whose difficulty is an enduring self-accusation, if you are unwilling or unable to forgive yourself, then let me ask you a number of questions.

I.   *Is your sense of guilt appropriate?*

God knows we have enough real sins to repent of without inventing other sins to torment us. Yet that is what we sometimes do. We waste a great deal of valuable emotional energy by taking far too seriously trivial conceits of our own which we regard as sins, and allowing them to make us feel guilty. If instead of feeling guilty about them we were to spend our energy gaining insight into them, we might well discover that something other than a sense of guilt is more appropriate. We might discover that laughter, anger or compassion are more fitting; not only wiser and healthier, but also closer to the truth of things. Let me give you instances of what I mean.

I know some who are trying to forgive themselves for behaviour they regard as sinful, but which any wise assessment should regard as innocent and trivial. I was brought up to believe, for example, that Christians should not go to the cinema, that it was wrong to see any film. Well, not *any* film; almost any film. It was permissible to see anything that had Shirley Temple in it.

Smoking was another "sin." If ever there was a saint it was my father, but there were some Christians who were a little unsure of the genuineness of his faith just because he loved his pipe. Their own censorious spirit troubled their conscience not a bit, but they regarded this loving, generous man as "suspect" because he liked to smoke.

Dancing was evil. I still can't do it. I may have the melody in my head and the rhythm in my heart, but I can't get them into my feet. The problem is theological. As soon as anyone sees me on the dance floor they recognize at once that I am a man with a theological problem. It is declared in every movement of my sideways shuffle which I attempt to adapt to all beats and rhythms.

To use make-up was held to be wicked. Women who took faith seriously did not wear lipstick or have their hair done. They thought they were insincere if they were not looking their worst. Put all this together and it was a perfectly adequate definition to say that a Christian was a person who didn't smoke, didn't dance and didn't go to the cinema. Of course, laughter is the proper response to such triviality. But there was a time when some of us did not laugh at these peccadilloes; we felt guilty about them. We are wiser now. We have a better sense of what really matters, both in life and in faith. And now, instead of having a sense of guilt when we review those particular "sins," we laugh at them.

Sometimes we spend energy trying to deal with a sense of guilt that is ours only because of an over-scrupulous conscience. Our conscience needs careful watching. It can become a tyrant, majoring in minors and driving us mad by being far too sensitive. Not long ago I heard of a man who went to a baseball game at Fenway Park, Boston. During the course of the game a batter hit a foul ball which went high in the air and dropped into the man's hands. He put it in his pocket and took it home. Now, part of the fun of the game is to catch a ball that is hit into the crowd and keep it as a souvenir. The ball clubs encourage spectators to do this, and say so in their official programs. In spite of this, the man's conscience began to bother him until he couldn't bear its accusation any longer. He wrote a letter to the management at Fenway Park explaining what he had done and enclosing the price of a baseball. The administration was very wise. The man received a brief note which said, "Don't be silly! Put your conscience to better use!"

Some of us are trying to deal with a sense of guilt that has been with us since we were children. Do you remember how, when you were a child, you felt responsible and blamed yourself for nearly every unhappy thing that happened? You were vulnerable and could feel guilty about almost anything. I am told that the children of divorced parents often feel that the divorce is their fault. Little ones who have been sexually abused often feel guilty about the experience as though *they* had done something wicked. When I was a little boy, I injured my thumb. I held it folded into the palm of my hand and closed my hand tight, not because the injury was painful, or to protect it, but because, somehow, I was ashamed of it.

I know a woman who went to hear an itinerant preacher and was convinced by him that what you and I might call an unsatisfactory habit was in fact an unpardonable sin. As a result, she lived for forty years in a deep sense of God's rejection of her. When we are young it is easy for others to make us feel guilty, and sometimes that childhood sense of wrong is allowed to pervade our adult life.

Some of us feel guilty by hindsight. We look back at some mistake we made and judge it as though we knew as much then as we know now. To do so is to treat ourselves unfairly, but we do it anyway and keep on doing it. We insist on carrying this burden of vain regret as though we were as wise and mature when we did the foolish thing as we are now. But we are thirty years older, and a little wiser. We should know better than to keep on blaming ourselves for mistakes we made by not having an old head on young shoulders. Of course it was foolish to do what we did; but some things are learned only by experience, and that is something we don't have a great deal of when we're young. Someone said once that only fools learn by experience. But there are some lessons that are hard to learn in any other way. We should be comforted by the wise words of Kierkegaard, "Life is lived forward but it is only understood backwards." We must learn to make allowances for ourselves.

Further, some of us have never had the experience of being unconditionally loved; rather, love was something we had to deserve or earn. Of course, once you see it like that you never can be sure that you have done enough to deserve or earn it. And we carried that sense of not being good enough into our adult life. I know husbands and wives who are still trying to earn and deserve the affection of their life's partner, and children who are not sure of the love of their parents. If you love your children, tell them. Leave no doubts. Let them know that they are loved, not only when they're good, but when they're bad and need it more. Convey to them the assurance and confidence that they are loved unconditionally. Love for husband or wife or child is not something awarded at the end because it is deserved or earned, but something bestowed at the beginning, a gift we delight to give and has only to be received.

Philip Larkin, one of the best of recent British poets, speaks about the sense of wrongness that permeates the lives of so many of us. Asking why this should be so, he answers that life's wrongness comes over us chiefly as a sense of all that we could have done had we been loved. Nothing cures that ache, he tells us. There is little joy in trying to make yourself acceptable and never being sure whether or not you've been able to do it. What a difference it makes when you know that you are loved deeply, unconditionally, unreservedly!

Sometimes our sense of guilt goes back to an unrealistic and limitless expectation that was made of us when we were small. I remember when our children brought their report card home from school, proud of their little accomplishment, I would look at it with its near-perfect score and say, "So you've failed again, have you?" And their eyes would shine and their faces glow at my mock displeasure, so full of love and tenderness. They would enter into the spirit of the game, and pretend to be sad and solemnly promise to do better next time. It was a way of loving them, and they knew it. But I know a woman whose father would be angry with her because she had achieved only ninety-eight percent when she might have had one-hundred. And it was no pretended displeasure. What had happened to the other two percent, he would ask angrily. The little girl would wilt under his scorn, and carried that sense of failure and of never being quite good enough into womanhood. Always she felt guilty and inferior, however well she did. She was never able to please him, and never knew what it was to be delighted and elevated by his pleasure in her.

Sometimes we know a sense of guilt because we burden ourselves with an endless expectation. Think of the questions we ask ourselves at three o'clock in the morning when, as Scott Fitzgerald tells us, it is always the dark night of the soul. We wonder if we loved our children enough, or if we were kind enough to our parents. And then we begin to dwell on the things we might have done had we loved them perfectly, and soon we have a sense of failure both as children and as parents.

We should realize that if we ask questions of that sort, we can't win. They are mischievous, endless, profitless. Of course we could have loved our parents more; of course we could have done more for our children. No matter how much we did or how deeply we loved, we could have done more and loved more. But it is foolish to dwell on things done and left undone. We loved them and were loved by them, and our love was the meaning of their life and ours. There is nothing to feel guilty about in that, but much for which to be thankful. Ask openended questions of that sort and you will always feel a failure.

Is your sense of guilt appropriate? Instead of too readily accepting the guilt we feel, we should try to gain insight into it. If we do so, we'll sometimes find that a sense of humour, compassion or indignation, is a healthier and truer way to deal with our experience. Sometimes we need to understand ourselves more than we need to forgive ourselves.

II.   *Are you still trying to justify yourself?*

Here we come to a basic misunderstanding of what forgiveness is. We remember some wrong we have done, some sin we have committed, and think that self-forgiveness would be possible if only we could explain to ourselves why we did it. Or we think that God would forgive us if only we could find a rational explanation for our wrong-doing. We look for an excuse, believing that if we could find one, forgiveness would be possible. We forget that if our behaviour can be excused it does not need to be forgiven. Forgiveness is not a way of dealing with what is excusable, but with what is inexcusable. If we can explain our wrong-doing, then we don't need to be forgiven, we just need to be understood. Forgiveness becomes a way of justifying ourselves, of saying that if only we were good enough, God would forgive us and we could forgive ourselves. But if we were good enough, God would not need to forgive us, and we should not need to forgive ourselves. It is when what we have done is inexcusable, beyond reason and explanation, that we most need to have forgiveness, both God's and our own.

Never a month goes by but I receive a letter from some bank or trust company offering to lend me money or to increase the amount of money I can borrow. The thing I notice about these magnanimous offers is that they are made to people who don't need to borrow money. Where were they when we were poor? It was different when we really did need to borrow money and went to see our bank manager about it. We came away feeling that he was a very fine friendly fellow indeed and would have been delighted to lend us enormous amounts of money once we had demonstrated that we did not need it. When we can secure our loan with an equal amount to guarantee it, who needs it?

Our thinking about forgiveness is like that. We are sure that God will forgive us if we can excuse our wrong-doing well enough to show that we don't need His forgiveness. Someone asked me the other day what we are to do with what is unforgiveable.The answer is that we are to forgive it. It is the only way to deal with it. It's not when we are good, or perfect, or when our behaviour is understandable and excusable that we need to be forgiven. It's when we have been a terrible disappointment to ourselves and others, when we have no excuses to offer, when our attempts at rationalizing are empty even to us and we have no claim but the claim of our need, that forgiveness begins to mean something. Then it is our only hope. So don't keep on trying to justify yourself. Forgiveness means that you are justified. Don't keep on trying to explain and excuse the wrongs you've done. Forgiveness is ours when we are without excuse. That is the nature and wonder of it.

III.   *If you are having difficulty forgiving yourself, is it because you haven't tried to put right what is wrong?*

I know people who spend an enormous amount of energy trying to forgive themselves for some wrong they have done when one simple, single act of restitution would put the whole thing right.

I know a man who owes a friend of mine fifty dollars. He has owed it to him for fifteen years. The indebtedness means nothing to my friend. It is to him a paltry sum of money. He doesn't need it and would be happy to forget it. Except that at least twice a year this man tells my friend, "I haven't forgotten the money I owe you!" He replies, "Forget it! I have!" But no! Six months later he is greeted with, "I haven't forgotten the money I owe you!" It goes on endlessly.

Now, if I were in that man's position, I would either pay my debt or take my friend at his word and forget it. But it's silly and annoying to go on mentioning the indebtedness and do nothing to pay it off. One simple, single act of restitution would settle the matter forever. But no, it drags on and on until it has become a joke.

We can hardly believe the story, it is so foolish; but we do the same thing ourselves without noticing the foolishness. We feel guilty because we have neglected our friends. Don't feel guilty about your neglect of them, write them a letter of friendship! We regret an estrangement that has gone on too long. Don't waste energy on regret if what is called for is an apology! We feel guilty that we have done so little to help those who are afflicted. Don't feel guilty, go and visit them, or write a cheque to comfort them! The truth is that some of us would rather keep on confessing our debts than pay them.

This can cut very close to the bone. Sometimes we have difficulty forgiving ourselves because we keep on doing the things for which we need to forgive ourselves. We persist in the actions and attitudes that are the cause of our distress. What we find hard to forgive is not merely the wrong we do but our unwillingness to give it up. We intend to keep on doing it, and therefore find it hard to forgive it. Some of us are caught up in relationships, or habits, or business practices that make us uneasy. We arc uncomfortable about them, but are not sure what to do about them, or are unwilling to do what we know we ought to do. In such circumstances it is hard to find peace. There may be no clear answer, no simple solution. Whatever we do will bring deep hurt to someone.

I hope you don't feel abandoned in your dilemma. I hope you will believe that God's gracious Spirit, the Spirit of Wisdom, Truth and Love, is present with you in it, guiding you to the place of insight and strengthening you in the place of decision. In your predicament you must not feel that God is against you, or that His only function is to judge and condemn you. He wills for you what you, in your best moments, will for yourself; and He will help you discover what that is. Then He will bring you through with grace and integrity.

It may be of some comfort to you to know that such experiences are not unknown even to the saints. St. Augustine had a mistress who bore him a child. But having a mistress afflicted his conscience, and a sense of guilt troubled him. He asked God to deliver him, praying that He would take her away. Then he added to his prayer the words, "only not yet!"

IV. *Is your reluctance to forgive yourself a kind of moral snob-bery, a spiritual elitism that is death to the soul?*

It is astonishing the varied forms this takes. Some people boast of their sins and, having enormously exaggerated them, are persuaded they are so great that not even God could for-give them!

Have you ever been to a testimony meeting at which people publicly confess the sins they have committed? Meetings of this sort were common in the church during the early years of my ministry. Sometimes I had the impression that confession was a kind of competition. A modest confession would be made, but might be treated with contempt by the next speaker. His attitude declared, "What a poor little sin that was! Just lis-ten to this big one!" Years ago Leslie Weatherhead was com-missioned by a religious journal to attend a meeting at which people attempted to be perfectly honest about their wicked-ness. He came back and wrote an amusing article in which he confessed that he had found the meeting fascinating, for he had discovered seven new sins and eleven new temptations. What an upside-down kind of pride, what an inordinate con-ceit it is that leads us to boast of such sinfulness that not even God can forgive it!

Dr. Russel Maltby was once approached by a woman who claimed a wickedness so great that not even God could forgive her. He told her that if she were to speak like that to God He would reply, "Nonsense, my dear woman! I had a far more dif-ficult case than yours only this morning!" Listen:

> Once in a saintly passion I cried with desperate grief,
> Ah! Lord! my heart is black with guile, of sinners I am chief.
> Then stooped my guardian angel and whispered from behind,
> "Vanity! my little man, you're nothing of the kind!"

No sin you have ever committed is so heinous that God can-not forgive it. None of us is ever beyond the reach of His mercy. Not even you!

Here is another of our conceits. Sometimes we feel superior to people who are able to forgive themselves. We are not like them. We have such a heightened moral perception, are so spiritually refined and feel such abhorrence for what we have done, that we could not possibly forgive ourselves. Less sensitive people might be able to do it, but not us.

If that is how you are tempted to think of yourself, then I tell you that you must stop playing games that are hazardous to the health of your soul. Spiritual refinement does not mean spiritual snobbery, it means believing the love God has for us and the grace He offers us. We all live by grace, and because we do, the difference in the eyes of God between a good man and a bad man is insigificant, as Reinhold Niebuhr has told us so clearly and so often. And this is true, not because sin is unimportant, but because we are all sinners. Indeed, there is grace enough to forgive even our spiritual snobbery by breaking through the conceit of it and giving in its place a humble, penitent, believing gladness.

Ministers of religion need to hear this word and to take it to heart, for sometimes those of us who preach God's redeeming grace to others cannot believe that we may also be the recipients of it. We have a double standard, not only for the wrongs we commit — imagining that our sins are worse than anybody else's — but for the grace we preach, believing that it is for everyone except us. That, too, is a conceit. We are neither better nor worse than others, and there is mercy even for professional holy men and women like us. Preachers, too, live by grace.

V.   *That brings me to the last point I want to make. Many of us cannot forgive the wrongs we have done to dear ones who are now dead.*

They are now beyond our reach. We cannot apologize to them, or explain to them, or ask their forgiveness. We have a deep sense of helpless guilt.

Here is a person who laments that when her father died he was in New York and she was in California. By the time she arrived at his bedside, he was unconscious, and there was no way that the estrangement could be reconciled, the explanation offered, the forgiveness received. We think of things we might have done for our parents and wish we could have their pardon for not having done them. But we cannot, for they are dead.

I think of Samuel Johnson standing in the rain in Lichfield, drenched to the skin, in an act of penitence for things he might have done, but hadn't done, to help his father. I remember old Thomas Carlyle, so unkind and insensitive to his wife Jane while she was alive, and so tormented with remorse when she died. He cried out that he would gladly surrender the whole world to have her back for five minutes to tell her that he loved her even though he had treated her so badly. But it was too late. How could he tell her, and how could he receive her forgiveness, when she was gone from him for ever? It is an anguish as old as time and as deep as life.

It is a thought full of truth, strength and comfort to remember that our dear ones, whom we may have wronged and who are now in Glory, love us more, not less, than they did when they walked with us here below. They understand us better, not worse. They themselves see more clearly than they ever saw on earth, how much they themselves have been forgiven; and what can that do but deepen their sympathy and compassion? Their pardon of us is but the overflow of the gratitude they feel for all they have been forgiven.

Remember, too, that we may well be grieving their spirits by not believing that they have forgiven us. If I am certain of anything it is that my parents, both of whom are dead, would be wounded if I did not live in the joy of the love and forgiveness they bear me; even as I should be deeply grieved to think that my children could doubt for a moment the love and acceptance I have for them. The spirits of our blessed dead must wonder how we could think so poorly of them as not to believe the love and forgiveness in which they hold us.

So it is with you and those whom you have loved long-since and lost awhile. They have forgiven you already, and in the wonder of the grace you have received, you will make God's heart glad, and their joy complete, by forgiving yourself.

REMEMBERING TO FORGET

To forgive others is difficult; but those of a generous nature and introspective temperament often find it harder to forgive themselves. By their largeness of spirit they forgive others over and over again, for they are too magnanimous to bear a grudge for long. Yet often they do not treat themselves so kindly. Their sensitivity can make them introspective, given to self-doubt and self-accusation, more prone to find added faults in themselves than to forgive the failings they have already found and upon which they continue to dwell.

In an earlier sermon we examined this tendency to self-blame, attempting to gain insight into its nature and to see it in a clear and wise perspective. Here I want to ask you three questions which will immediately place any insight we have gained in a larger setting, that of our relationship to God and other people.

I. *Have you received the forgiveness of God?*

Dr. Austin Farrer, Warden of Keble College, Oxford, was, until his untimely death in 1968 at the age of sixty-two, one of the most brilliant philosophers and theologians of our time, with the gift and discipline to say profound things in a simple way. When he spoke of forgiveness he told how, when he was a child at school, a teacher wrote a humiliating remark in his copybook. It stayed there until the book had been filled with lessons, and then, following the custom of the school, was taken home to be scrutinized by parents.

The little boy could not bring himself to take home and hand over the unhappy book. He could not bear to have his parents read the contemptuous comment. On the way home from school he tore out the page and buried it in a ditch. Then he discovered that to tear out one page left another one loose, so that one also had to come out and be buried. That done, it meant that the writing on yet another page began in the middle of a sentence and so made no sense at all. Yet he brought the book home and, blushing, handed it over to his mother.

That night he slept hardly at all, and when he did, his sleep was troubled. In his dreams, neighbours arrived at the front door waving the buried pages, dug up from the leafy earth, still damp and stained. This was worse than anything he had imagined. The whole unhappy episode was getting out of hand.

The wee fellow could stand it no longer. Next morning he called his mother to his bedside and with three sobs to every sentence confessed the sad story, only to find that when he was but half-way through it, her arms were around him in love and acceptance. The relief of it! The joy of having nothing to conceal! To look at his dear parents with affection unspoiled by guilt seemed to him the supreme happiness. He never forgot it. The experience was for ever after the starting point of his understanding of God's forgiveness of us.

A theologian, speaking one day to his friend Leslie Weatherhead, told him how as a small child he had disobeyed his mother and had been sent to his room to await punishment by his father when he came home. Later, he heard his father's key in the lock, the opening and closing of the front door, the sounds of greeting and the muffled conversation as, he supposed, the story of his wickedness was told. He waited until he could bear waiting no longer. It seemed better to meet judgment half way, and so he made his way cautiously out of his room and down the stairs. Just as he reached the bottom step his father appeared, caught sight of him, and ran quickly to gather him up in his arms with the words, "My own wee son!"

The little boy never forgot it. As an adult he could not tell the story without tears coming to his eyes. He said to his friend, "I shall never forget the delicious sense of *belonging* to my father." The experience became his way into a deep understanding of God's forgiveness of us.

And now my own confession; and confession it is! Behind the dresser in the bedroom of the house in which I grew up, the wallpaper didn't quite fit into the sharp corner of the wall. I need not explain the details to you, but I discovered that I could push my finger through it, and that the sensation was pleasant and satisfying (like hitting a good clean shot at golf). I could not resist doing it over and over again. The marks were not easily seen, for they were behind the dresser. The trouble was that, seen or not, I knew they were there, and the thought of them was a shadow on my days and the torment of my nights.

They bothered me most when life was most blissful. To put it in an Irish sort of way, it was when I was happiest that I was most unhappy. And then there came a day when the sun was warm, the skies blue, and the flowers fragrant. My mother never looked more beautiful, and life was ecstasy. Except that there were holes in the wallpaper behind the dresser. I couldn't bear it any longer. I shall never forget the relief of tears, the tenderness that held and reassured me, and how in one sentence of acceptance, Eden was restored and paradise regained.

Do you remember what it was like to be forgiven; no longer to feel guilty and inferior, with a dreadful sense of having shut yourself off from joy? If you do, you have your best clue to God's forgiveness of us, for the stories I have told you are not only full of sentiment, they are deep with truth.

For one thing, they teach us that if we are penitent, it is because the goodness of God makes us so. How can we bear to deceive, or disobey, or close ourselves out from such kindness? No doubt the television evangelist is right when he promises that if we repent, God will forgive us. But how do we repent? What makes us ashamed and sorry for the wrong we have done? I used to be told that God's anger would frighten me into repentance, but that never was my experience. My feeling was that I could not bear to wound such love, to allow any deed of mine to cloud such beauty of kindness. The truth for me is that He has loved me into loving, smiled me into smiling, forgiven me into repentance. It was God's goodness that made me sorry for my sins, not His anger. It was His "My own wee son!" that made me feel the pity of allowing anything to diminish that intimacy.

Another truth the stories teach us is that God does not

merely forgive our sins, He forgives *us*. There is a sense in which sins cannot be forgiven, only people can. And if we speak of God's forgiveness, we must mean His forgiveness not of this sin or that sin, but of you and me and all our sins. Forgiveness is not for what we have done, merely, but for what we are. And that means that *we* are forgiven. Our penitence is more than a moment of regret over a particular sin; it is the offering of ourselves to God, with all our imperfections, knowing that we are accepted for His love's sake. God's forgiveness of us is not a matter of isolated moments, of fits and starts; it is a dimension in which we live and move and have our being. We breathe it as we breathe the air; we turn our face towards it as we turn to the sun; we bathe in it as we bathe in the ocean. Indeed, those are Whitman's words, "Bathe me, O God, in Thee." One of our great theologians tells us that forgiveness is "a ceaseless flow of loving acceptance."

Yet another insight our stories yield is that what forgiveness gives back to us is a person. To be forgiven is to be restored to the joy of a relationship whose happiness was clouded by our wrong-doing. Farrer's confession restored his mother to him. The father's forgiveness was declared in his claiming his child as "my own wee son," and received by the little boy as a "delicious sense of belonging." Forgiveness restores people to us and us to them. God's forgiveness of us is a loving relationship graciously restored.

Further, the stories speak to us of the *completeness* of God's forgiveness. Have you noticed that one lie can make the whole world false? One act of deception and the sun no longer shines, the birds no longer sing, and everything is less than it once was because we are false. To crooks, everything is crooked. Everything and everybody must be crooked to them, for they are crooked themselves. But if one false word can make the whole world false, one word of forgiveness can give the whole thing back to us, complete and restored to all its truth and integrity.

Sometimes, in our smallness, we forgive reluctantly and set limits to our forgiveness. We say that we will forgive but not forget; and that is no forgiveness at all, for the forgiveness that remembers is a poor, half-hearted thing, hardly worthy of the name. The true thing is complete. That is what the Bible means when it says that God "will forgive their iniquity *and remember their sin no more.*" Nothing is more complete than a deliberate intention to forget. That is why Paul Tillich wonderfully describes forgiveness by saying that it is the past that is remembered that it may be forgotten. There is no pretence about this forgiveness. It does not deceive itself. It sees clearly and knows truly. It does not pretend that what happened did not happen. It knows that it did happen, and faces it, and remembers it that it may be forgotten.

George MacDonald puts it another way in one of his prayers:

> I prayed to God that He would make me into a rock which swallowed up the waves of wrong in its great caverns and never threw them back to swell the commotion of the angry sea whence they came. Ah, what it would be actually to annihilate wrong in this way, to be able to say, "It shall not be wrong against me, so utterly do I forgive it."

That is what God does. His forgiveness is so complete that "He remembers our sin no more." And, as one of the saints reminds us, "what God has forgotten, 'tis no business of ours to remember."

So don't go on confessing the same sin and pleading for forgiveness for it over and over again. Many of our prayers of confession ought to be prayers of thanksgiving for the forgiveness we have received. Remember that God is not reluctant to forgive us, but more willing to forgive us than we are either to ask or receive His pardon. Indeed, our asking is the work of His Spirit in us, for He has accomplished all our repentance. You are forgiven! You dwell in a forgiven universe! You don't need to plead for what is graciously offered! Believe it, accept it, and live in the joy of it!

II.   *Have you forgiven others?*

We know, because we know The Lord's Prayer, that the

condition of God's forgiveness of us is our willingness to forgive other people. "And forgive us our trespasses, as we forgive
those who trespass against us" we pray every time we say The
Lord's Prayer. It sounds like a bargain, a nicely calculated
arrangement, a workable contract. God seems to say, "You forgive others and I'll forgive you." Except that what looks like a
conditional promise is really an impossible demand. "Forgive
those who need your forgiveness and I'll forgive you," God
seems to say. But when the disciples heard that, their reply was
immediate and desperate: "Increase our faith!" We don't have
it in us to forgive as we should; how then are we to have the
forgiveness of God? What at first glance looks like a fair
request is in fact a disheartening and impossible expectation.

I want to tell you about my ring. It is the only ring I've ever
seen that I ever wanted to wear, and it is very old. It was given
to me twenty years ago by an elderly woman who was a member of my church in Sarnia. She came to see me one day to tell
me that while she loved the church and attended its services
regularly, she found little comfort in its message. Our Lord
seemed to say, "If you do not forgive others, I will not forgive
you." She went on to tell me that her father had done things to
her which she could not forgive. What he had done had
warped and crippled her life and spoiled her happiness. But if
she did not forgive her father, God would not forgive her. No
assurance of pardon promised in worship, therefore, ever
reached her. She longed for that assurance, but believed that it
was not for her. God would not forgive her until she had forgiven her father, and that was more than she could manage;
she didn't have it in her to do it. The assurance of pardon was
a message for someone else, not for her. She envied those who
could accept it with confidence and live in it with joy.

Now, in every congregation of which I have been the minister, and in quite a few in which I have preached, there has
been at least one person like that. I mention this lady only
because she made her difficulty so clear, and because she
became so dear to me. What would you have said to her, or to
others like her?

Let me tell you what I said: I told her that God's forgiveness of us and our forgiveness of others are not two things, but one; that God is not set over against us making an impossible demand, but with us, enabling us by His grace to do what we cannot do by ourselves; that His forgiveness of us is the very power that enables us to forgive others!

When I said that to her, she replied that it sounded almost too good to be true. She would have to think about it. And so she did, for several days. Then she called me, sounding like a new woman. The burden had been lifted. Not only did she know a wonderful sense of God's acceptance, but in the grace and joy of it she had begun to forgive her father. A little later we went together into the sanctuary and renewed our vows of membership in the Body of Christ. My ring was her gift to me. Every time I look at it, I am reminded of the grace of God that enables us to do what we cannot do by ourselves.

Saint Augustine puts it splendidly in a prayer: "Demand what Thou wilt, but first give me that which Thou dost demand!" God will not ask us to forgive anyone without granting us the grace to do it; and the more we grow in the spiritual life the more we will realize that God's forgiveness of us and our forgiveness of other people are really one and the same thing. If I have been forgiven by God, how can I withhold my forgiveness from you? If I live by grace, how can I not be gracious? If I live by the divine mercy, must I not be merciful?

God's forgiveness of us and our forgiveness of others are but one thing in yet another sense. Suppose you have treated me unjustly and made me resentful. Two things now need to be dealt with — your unfairness and my bitterness. But if, by God's grace, I forgive the wrong done me, does not that act of forgiveness deal also with the lovelessness of my resentment? Forgiving you, my hostility is gone. One single act has dealt with both your wrong and my resentment of it, and that one act of pardon is the action of God's grace in my heart, enabling me to forgive.

To put it another way, how can we begin to believe in God's forgiveness of us if we do not forgive those who have wronged us? Do you know why we find it hard to believe that God has forgiven us? It is because we are so reluctant to forgive others. We think God must be reluctant too. If we forgave more, and more completely, the very experience of doing so would make it easier for us to believe God's forgiveness of us.

What is it you need to forgive? An old wrong that has been brooded over for years? Some betrayal, some hurt inflicted, some offence against love and trust, some estrangement that has closed out of your life a person whom you very much want to be in it? That is not beyond the reach of God's grace and yours. He can do something with it. He can enable *you* to do something with it.

III.   *If you have received the forgiveness of God, and if by His grace you are able to forgive others, then why have you not forgiven yourself?*

In other words, why can you not show to yourself the mercy God has already shown to you, and you have already shown to others? Do you think you know better than He? He thinks you are forgivable, for He has forgiven you. Do you wish to argue the matter with Him? Are you wiser than God, or more spiritually perceptive? If *He* has forgiven you, what is holding you back? "If God be for us, who can be against us?" Paul asks in his greatest rhetorical question. God's mercy has been given to you; why can you not have mercy on yourself?" God knows you completely, far better than you know yourself. He made you, and makes you, and by His Spirit understands you at the depth of your inarticulate groans. When all that we can utter is a sigh we do not understand, God knows what our sighing means, and accepts and forgives us at that deep level. But if this is so, no knowledge that we have of ourselves must be allowed to convince us that we are beyond forgiveness. God, in His forgiveness of us, has taken every dark secret into account! God has forgiven us, and there can be no appeal from Him to anyone higher. Not even to ourselves.

Again, if you have forgiven others, why will you not extend the same kindness to yourself that you have shown to them? Generous in forgiving others, why are you so mean in withholding forgiveness from yourself? Show your own self the mercy God has shown you and the kindness you have extended to others. That is His commandment: "Love thy neighbour as thyself." But that also means loving ourselves as we love our neighbour! And if we love our neighbour enough to be willing to forgive him the wrongs he has done us, perhaps we should love ourselves enough to forgive the wrongs we have done.

To put it another way: what if someone who had wronged you came to you with genuine sorrow for the wrong they had done, asking your forgiveness and seeking your acceptance? What would you think of yourself if you not only refused to pardon them, but did everything in your power to make them feel more miserable, inferior, and guilty than before? What if you sought them out when they were most vulnerable, when they were tired or emotionally drained, and reminded them of their treachery and failure? What kind of person would you think yourself to be?

Leslie Weatherhead's mother did that to her son. When he had offended her in some childish way she would deliberately withhold forgiveness from him until the little boy would be desperate with grief and guilt. We think her cruel for what she did, and wonder what dark power in her own life moved her to do so. Yet that is what we do to ourselves. Not content merely to withhold our forgiveness, we torture ourselves in the wee small hours of the morning, when it is so easy to feel worthless, by remembering the wrongs we have done to others. What an endless, profitless thing to do! How can we treat ourselves so cruelly?

If you have received the forgiveness of God, and if you have forgiven others, why have you not forgiven yourself? Are you afraid that it might be presumptuous of you to do so? But He will teach us that He may be trusted even with our fears, and to the very end He will assure and reassure us of His mercy. This is expressed beautifully in the last verse of Donne's great *Hymn to God The Father*:

> I have a sin of fear, that when I have spun
> My last thread, I shall perish on the shore;
> But swear by Thyself, that at my death Thy Son
> Shall shine as He shines now, and heretofore:
> And, having done that, Thou hast done,
> I fear no more.

THE ATTRACTIVENESS OF FAILURE

St. John 5:6

The words of our text were spoken by Jesus to a man who had been ill for thirty-eight years and was lying, with many others, at the pool of Bethesda in Jerusalem. Our Lord asked him the question, "Do you want to recover?"

Now that's a very odd question, isn't it? The man had been ill for thirty-eight years and Jesus asked him if he wanted to be healed! But it is not odd; it is perceptive, for we know that sometimes our illness is a way of escaping from life without losing face. We hate to admit, "I am not up to it." Instead we say, "I can't do it. I am ill." We even do it unconsciously, so that nowdays we talk about psychosomatic illness. That just means that people are sometimes physically ill for reasons that have more to do with their health of mind or spirit than with any physical cause. He is a brave person indeed who will dare to mark the boundary between mind and body in matters of sickness and health. "Do you want to recover?" our Lord asks, and His question is not silly; it is perceptive, and by the insights of modern psychology we know that now better than we have ever known it.

Here is a marriage counselor who asks the couple he is trying to help, "Do you want to recover?" He knows that unless both partners want their marriage to survive, it probably won't. The first step on the way to recovery is to *want* to recover. Do you *want* to lose weight? Do you *want* to stop smoking? William James used to talk even about "the will to believe." Do you *want* to believe? Some of us do not. We have no desire to believe because to believe may be unsettling. Years ago Paul Scherer pointed out to us that if we allow ourselves to believe

44

that the universe has a purpose, it might mean that our lives should have one too, and that can be very disturbing.

The question instructs even our morality. St. Augustine had a mistress whom he loved but who troubled his conscience. So he asked God to take away his desire for her, and then added to his prayer the words, "But not yet!"

Do you want to recover? There are some people who have been grieving for years because they don't want to recover from their grief. There are some who have remained in a crippling sense of guilt for years because they don't want to be forgiven. Why? Because sometimes the dark side of our life, our shadow, our "failure," is not our problem but our solution. Some of us wouldn't know who we are if we didn't have a sense of guilt or grief. We allow ourselves to be defined by our dark side. I know a person, for example, who is always grumbling, always complaining; and if he stopped complaining he would immediately have a crisis of identity. His complaining has shaped and defined him to such a degree that he doesn't know he is doing it. It is just *him*.

How about you and me? Is our dark side our problem so that we want to be healed, or is it our solution so that we have no wish to recover? In other words, the negative part of us — the inferior, cowardly part, the failing part of us — has a certain attractiveness. It is a siren song that sings and holds us in its cruel enchantment and often leads us to disaster. Yet we so feel the power of its attractiveness that we don't want to escape from it. Why is it so?

I.   *Failure is attractive because it is easy.*

Jesus said to the paralyzed man, "Take up your bed and walk!" But the man hadn't had to do that for thirty-eight years. Someone else had taken up his bed, and not only his bed, but him as well; he hadn't had to walk because he had been carried! Sometimes the attractiveness of failure is simply that it is easier to fail than to succeed. Failure sometimes means that we are carried. Success is hard to achieve and may be a heavy burden to carry.

Think for a moment of those qualities that are necessary to success, and notice that they are all demanding and difficult. Each one of them carries its difficulty in its definition. What are the qualities? Courage is one of them; but courage is never easy. The same is true of fortitude, discipline, restraint, persistence, patience. All of these qualities are difficult. It is much easier to lapse into self-pity than to be brave; to settle for sympathy rather than to win admiration; to be a coward rather than a hero. That is the attractiveness of failure. It is easier.

We have a wonderful example of this in the parable of the prodigal son (St. Luke 15). When the young fellow returned from the far country he had already prepared the speech he would deliver to his father. He said, "Father I have sinned against heaven and in thy sight and am no more worthy to be called thy son. Make me as one of thy hired servants." Now, that's very neat, isn't it? He had already decided on his limited obligations. Back from wasteful living, the life of a servant was attractive because it was safe in its limitations.

But the father won't have it! "No way!" says the father to his son's request. "I will not treat you like a slave when you are my son! Why would you wish to behave like a hired servant when you are the love of my heart and my house is your home? I will not let you off so easily!" So he has the best robe brought forth, and thus bestows a little dignity. "And put a ring on his finger!" he cries. That just means that the boy is still his heir. "And put shoes on his feet!" That means that he is no slave, but a son. Only slaves went barefoot. Sons wore shoes:

> I got shoes, you got shoes,
> All o' God's chillun got shoes.
> When I get to heab'n I'm goin' put on my shoes,
> I'm goin' walk all ovah God's heab'n.

Do you know why? Because heaven is home, and I am God's child. Indeed, I am not going to walk, I am going to dance in the joy of my Father's house.

All through Scripture you will find two complementary ideas of sin. One tells us that we are guilty of constantly overreaching ourselves, trying to be God, what Karl Barth once called our "Titanism," that overreaching of our humanity that denies our creatureliness. And always the first casualty of that kind of humanism is our humanity. But there is another view of sin. In this view it is not an overreaching of our humanity but a falling short of it. It is not being more than human, but less. It is missing the mark, failing to be what God meant us to be. We are sometimes told that nowdays we lack a sense of sin. I believe that to be untrue. I think I can give you a sense of sin in ten seconds, because if I speak the words you will recognize them as true. Sin is the difference between what we are and what we might have been. Now do you have "a sense of sin"? Is any of us unaware of that difference? Listen to an old prayer from the Hebrides:

> Take me often from the tumult of things into Thy presence;
> There show me what I am and what Thou hast purposed me to be.
> Then hide me from Thy tears.

Do you want to recover? We don't want to recover because it is easier not to.

The old infirmity lingers on even among Christian people who ought to know better. "I am only a sinner," we say. And the implication is that not much can be expected of a sinner. Except that in the Christian church there are no sinners, only *forgiven* sinners, and that's different. When we are forgiven sinners it means that we have moved from being guilty to being responsible, and that is a giant step towards maturity. That is to take the hard road to recovery. But however hard it is, it is the way to health.

II.   *Failure is attractive because it confirms our poor opinion of ourselves.*

Someone said once that we make up our minds very early in life what kind of person we are going to be, and spend the rest of our lives confirming it. There is something in that. The trouble is that if we make such a decision when we are children then we make up our mind about the kind of person we're going to be when we are smaller than everybody else. Everyone else is bigger, stronger and wiser than we are, and that makes it easy to start off with a sense of inferiority. That sense of inferiority is often strengthened by the insensitivity, foolishness or wickedness of other people. Parents, teachers, preachers can all confirm us in our inferiority. We know it, for we can all remember some such wound inflicted on us, and recognize some scar. And sometimes it is done even in the name of God.

A man talking to old Carlyle Marney, that magnificent Southern Baptist preacher, told him, "Marney, God is the worst thing that ever happened to me!" It is easy to know what he meant. Let me ask you: when you were growing up did you ever think that God really liked you, that He approved of you, that He delighted in you as your parents did and as you now delight in your own children? Did that ever occur to you, or are you among the many who grew up believing that God was against them; that He was always austere, disapproving; that He really didn't like them; that He demanded a perfection they had no hope of achieving? He was supremely the one-hun-dred-percenter so that there was no way they could meet His demands and *had* to feel a failure. So it is that many of us have gone through life with a deep sense of not really being any good. There were times when we thought we had overcome the feeling, that we had the victory over it; and then suddenly and unexpectedly we found ourselves in circumstances that threat-ened our self-esteem, and instantly the old inferiority was there in all its familiar power to cripple us. It whispered in our ear, when we least needed to hear it, that we were no good; that we had no hope of succeeding in any great enterprise; that we didn't *deserve* to succeed even if we could; that we were really a great fraud.

"Well," you reply, "what you are telling us may be true in other places, but not in New York. Don't you know that, being in New York, we are top of the heap, that we are the successful ones? No inferiority here, but confidence, aggressiveness, achievement! We know what we can do because we've done it!

We wouldn't be where we are if we hadn't!" And some of us *are* prominent, powerful and influential, aren't we? Except, of course, that our sense of inferiority doesn't pay any attention, or pays hardly any attention, to our accomplishments. It has little or nothing to do with them. The very fact that we must list our successes expresses our unease. Why do we have to tell ourselves so often that we're at the top? The man who says to me, "I am just as good as you," betrays himself. If he really thought he was he wouldn't need to say it! All our talk about our security just expresses our insecurity.

The New York Times tells us that seventy percent of all big executives, the movers and shakers in our country, have a sense of personal unworthiness, of guilt, of unease. For that reason, among others, some of them are giving up. Others put on a mask, adopt an image, play a part. Somebody said once that none of us is as good as we look; certainly none of us is as secure as we look. We're trying desperately to hide something that isn't even there — our emptiness. It is the sense of our own emptiness that frightens us. In spite of our appearance of competence, ease and sophistication, we are haunted by the sense that we're not up to it, that we can't do it, that it really is beyond us. Sometimes, to hide our emptiness, we begin to take ourselves too solemnly. We give ourselves airs in an attempt to persuade other people that we are far more assured than we are, in the hope that their deference will convince us that what we are trying to convince them of is true! But we are haunted by the certainty that the midnight hour will strike when all masks are off, and what will we be then?

It is often said that tragedy is ultimately more consoling than comedy because in tragedy we have faced the worst. Part of the attractiveness of failure is that when we have accepted it, we have faced the worst and can't fall any further. What a relief to accept our poor verdict on ourselves, and be reconciled to it! It is like the relief of a man struggling through a blizzard who yields to the awful temptation not to struggle any more, but to lie down and die. But the terrible thing is that to do so is death. And for you to accept your own poor estimate of yourself is to lose your true self needlessly, because your poor opinion of yourself is not true. Do you know why it isn't true? Because you have a value that doesn't depend on anything that you have either done or left undone. You have worth, not because of any accomplishment you have achieved, but because you are you, unique and unrepeatable. We are sometimes tempted to think that we are loved because we have value. The truth is we have value because we are loved.

Do you want security? Then find it in the place where children know it belongs, and that is in being loved. You don't have to put on a face, and you don't have to play a part, and you don't have to cultivate an image. The truth of you is better than any image you can project or any part you can play. It is that you are loved just as you are. Loved by God! Eternally! Unconditionally! Uniquely!

III.   *Failure is attractive because so often the risks of action are more apparent than the risks of inaction.*

That sounds difficult, so let me make it clear. Suppose for a moment that you are trying to make up your mind about some new venture. You wonder if you should do it. The prospect is frightening. If you attempt it, the risks are very great. You're not sure that you're up to the new demands it will make of you. You consider the course of action and all the risks are obvious at once, menacing, inhibiting. But sometimes it is a very good thing to ask yourself the question, not, "what are the risks if I do it?" but, "what am I in danger of losing if I don't?" The risks of action are often great and obvious; the risks of inaction may be greater still, *but they are often not so obvious*! Somebody said once that you either move forward or pay more to stay in the same place. How much more are you paying to stay in the same place? Have you even noticed what it is costing you to stay in the same place?

I was present once when a number of thoughtful men were discussing a business that was so successful that there was great pressure on them to expand it. Such expansion would not be easy. It would increase their costs and mean longer hours of work for busy executives. It would leave them more exposed and vulnerable than before. Over several months they had come together frequently to discuss the risks of expansion, only to be subdued by them. And then one man said, "If we do not expand then we must accept the fact that we have reached our limit. Is anyone prepared to do that?" No one was. There are dreadful risks in reaching your limit. The decision to expand was made and has since proved to be a wise one. They made their decision when they realized that while it may be frightening to launch out into uncharted waters, it may be fatal not to set sail at all.

Now I am going to cut very close to the bone. What about loving? That's a risky business. That is why many of the poets say it is not worth the hurt. Don't love anybody, because if you do you make yourself vulnerable. "He who hath wife and child hath given hostages to fortune!" And not wife and child only, but anyone to whom you have given your heart. Give your heart away and something terrible can happen to it. Someone may break it. Sidney Royse Lysaght warns us:

> If love should count you worthy, and should deign
> One day to seek your door and be your guest,
> Pause! ere you draw the bolt and bid him rest,
> If in your old content you would remain,
> For not alone he enters; in his train
> Are angels of the mist, the lonely guest
> Dreams of the unfulfilled and unpossessed,
> And sorrow, and Life's immemorial pain.
>
> He wakes desires you never may forget,
> He shows you stars you never saw before,
> He makes you share with him, for evermore,
> The burden of the world's divine regret.
> How wise you were to open not! and yet,
> How poor if you should turn him from the door!

But why is it sad to refuse love's entry if the risks of love are so great? Surely it is not sad, but prudent, to turn love away if to welcome it is so threatening. The answer is that while your heart will not be broken if you do not give it away, a far worse

thing may happen to it. It may become unbreakable. Like a
stone. And then all your love, all your tenderness, all your
grace and sympathy will die.

I think about this when I watch the sailboats on Lake
Huron and Georgian Bay where I love to be in the summer; or
when I go down to the bright waters of the Caribbean. The
lake and ocean are sometimes turbulent, and one fears for the
boat that is far from shore. Our fears, heightened by imagination, cry, "Don't go so far out! Come in! Stay close to land!"
That is what imagination says, but that is not what experience
knows. Our experience teaches us that when the seas are
stormy the one thing we need is good water under our keel.
Imagination may say it is safer to hug the shore, but experience knows the hazards of reefs and shallows. It is easy to see
the risks of sailing far out, but the risks of staying close in are
often greater, though not so obvious. And besides, if we stay
close to shore there is no voyage!

Do you want to recover? It is easier not to. But that is not
for you. You are better than that, aren't you? For you, only the
far horizons and the wide ocean and the mighty deep will do!
Listen to Walt Whitman:

> Sail forth! steer for the deep waters only!
> Reckless, O soul, exploring, I with thee and thou with me;
> For we are bound where mariner has not yet dared to go,
> And we will risk the ship, ourselves and all,
>
> O my brave soul!
> O farther, farther sail!
> O daring joy, but safe! Are they not all the seas of God?
> O farther, farther, farther sail.

"Do you want to recover?" He asked.
    Well, do you?

BORN AGAIN?

St. John 3:1–8

In His conversation with Nicodemus, Jesus said, "Unless a man has been born again, he cannot see the Kingdom of God." For some of us, that statement is the very heart of faith. We would describe ourselves as "born-again" Christians. For others, talk of being born again is a source of unease, perplexity and embarrassment. When someone asks us if we are born again, we hardly know how to reply.

When people ask me if I am born again, I find it a difficult question to answer. And finding it difficult, it's easy to believe that it must be because of some lack in me. If we cannot answer quickly and clearly, our faith must be uncertain. It's easy, then, to feel that our Christian experience is inferior to the faith of those who are sure of their answer.

I want to speak a word of reassurance to those who are perplexed in this way, and to do so by pointing out that the discomfort we feel is not necessarily because of the unsureness of our faith. It arises from the nature of the question, and even from the way it is asked. Some questions cannot be answered with an immediate, simple, "yes" or "no." If they are, the answer will be misleading. That is why we still make a joke of the old question, "Have you stopped beating your wife?" If we answer, "yes," we confess that we did beat her once but have happily abandoned the practice; and if we answer "no" we declare that we are still at it! The awkwardness of the simple "yes-or-no" question and answer is not found in our behaviour, but in the presupposition that shapes the question and gives it its silly form. The true answer to the question is that we never did beat our wife and the questioner is mistaken in

53

assuming that we did. Our mistake is in trying to answer the question before we have tidied it up.

Similarly, when someone asks me if I am born again, it seems the easiest thing in the world to answer with a simple "yes" or "no." In fact, I can't answer the question in that way for if I do my answer will be misleading.

If, for example, I say "yes," then the questioner will read into my answer all that *they* mean by being born again, and so I have satisfied them. But I am not at all happy about their interpreting my answer in their own way. They may have assumed too much. But if I say "no" then they may conclude from my answer that I am not a Christian, and that may be to assume too little. What we must do, then, is clarify what the question means so that our answer will lead to understanding rather than confusion. What, then, does it mean to be born again?

A good place to start is by asking what our Lord meant when He spoke to Nicodemus about the necessity of a new birth. It is clear at once that He was answering a question asked by Nicodemus concerning the Kingdom of God and how we may enter it. The answer to the question was "Unless a man is born again, he cannot see the Kingdom of God."

How to get into the Kingdom was a question frequently asked of our Lord, and He gave a number of answers to it. On more than one occasion He said that the way into the Kingdom is to become as a little child. Now, being told that I must be childlike in my dependence on God and in my trustfulness in God does not bother me as I am bothered when someone tells me that I must be born again. The words have a different tone to them. They are less a test to see whether my faith meets someone else's expectation and more an invitation to trust God as a little child trusts his father or mother.

If that is what it means to be born again, then I have no difficulty with it at all. This invitation to childlikeness is winsome. I covet the quality of it for myself and others. And, of course, it goes right to the heart of the Gospel and is one of the most startling statements our Lord ever uttered. No one had ever before elevated the child by declaring that childlikeness is the secret of the Kingdom; just as no one had ever dared to say that when we speak to God we should call Him "Abba." "Abba" is like our "mamma" or "dada." It is among the first words a baby is able to speak, and it means "daddy." To be childlike is to have the dependence, trust and affection that a little child feels for his father or mother. And to be born again is to be childlike. It is in this way that we enter the Kingdom of God.

Is that what the words mean to born-again Christians? For them they mean more than that and less than that, and it is this less and more that I want to search out and make explicit.

I. Notice, to begin with, that when we are asked if we are born again, the question is often made a test of the genuineness of our Christian experience. Only those who are born again possess authentic faith. If we cannot say that we are born again, we are not real Christians. The world is divided, then, into those who are born again and those who are not, and only those who are born again have the experience necessary to salvation. Faith, to be the real thing, must be experienced in this way, and expressed in these terms.

In the New Testament, however, this expression is only *one* way of expressing authentic faith. For one thing, in the New Testament it is mentioned in only one Gospel, the Gospel according to St. John. Nowhere in St. Matthew, St. Mark or St. Luke are we told that we must be born again. The words "born again" are mentioned in only one passage in St. John's Gospel, and this is the only Gospel in which they are mentioned. They are mentioned also in the First Epistle of John and in the First Epistle of Peter. Those are the only occasions in the New Testament. Our Lord was frequently asked about entering the Kingdom, about gaining eternal life, about how to become a disciple. And He answered in a great variety of ways. On only one occasion did He answer by saying that to enter the Kingdom we must be born again.

One day a rich young ruler came and asked, "What must I do to have eternal life?" Jesus did not say to him, "You must be born again"; He spoke of keeping the commandments and then appealed to him to sell his possessions and give the money away and come and follow Him. That was how our Lord issued His invitation to discipleship, His offer of eternal life.

When another young man came to Him and asked the same question, our Lord replied by telling him the story of the Good Samaritan. Jesus responded to his question by teaching him what it means to be a good neighbour and thus fulfill the secret of the two great commandments to love God with the whole heart and our neighbour as ourselves.

On yet another occasion when the matter was raised concerning those who had entered the Kingdom, He told the parable which declares that those who are recognized, accepted and pronounced righteous by God are the ones who have clothed the naked, fed the hungry and visited those who are in prison. He then went on to say that when the identity of the blessed is revealed there will be many surprises.

Do you understand what I am saying? Not for an instant am I denying that to speak of being born again is an authentic expression of Christian experience. I have several things to say in its favour. What I am saying to you now is that in the pages of the New Testament being born again is not the only way to express authentic Christian faith and discipleship. The early disciples were not known as born-again Christians. They were known simply as Christians, or in the very earliest days, as those who belonged to "The Way." I have not the slightest objection to the use of the term "born again" as *one* way of expressing our experience of forgiveness and reconciliation, but it is not the only way. The New Testament expresses the reality of faith in a great variety of ways, yet we have narrowed it down until this one way is the test of authentic faith. It seems to me to be an unhappy irony that the passage in John which speaks of the mystery and freedom of the Spirit should have become the passage which, more than any other, limits the work of the Spirit and the expression of authentic faith.

For instance, one day the telephone in my home rang and at the other end a woman told me that her mother was coming to live in London and was looking for a church that was "not apostate," that did not deny the truth of the Gospel. She had been told that my church was such a church and that we preached the true faith. But she wanted to be sure of it, and would like me to answer three or four questions to prove that I preached the Word. And first, she wanted to know if I was born again.

Now as soon as she asked the question, I had to decide how I was going to deal, not only with the question, but with her whole manner of approach and method of investigation. Did I want to continue the conversation? Should I tell her that I deplored the conceit that thought it could determine the quality of my faith and my church's Gospel by means of four quick questions on the telephone? Should I tell her to try her method on somebody else, not on me, and suggest another church she might call? Did I want to get into the whole matter with her?

I decided that I did, and began by telling her that I found her attitude disquieting and the tone of her question offensive. Did she really think that I was under some obligation to demonstrate the validity of my faith to her at any time, and in any circumstances, and by whatever standards she chose? And besides, I had a question of my own to ask. What would she say if, instead of my telling her whether or not I was born again, I told her I had been reconciled to God through Christ; that I had experienced the forgiveness of sins in Him; that I had turned to God with a trust which was itself the work of His grace; that I could not remember a time when I did not love God; that I knew the gracious work of His creative Spirit in my life; that any goodness there was in me was from Him who is the Fountain of all goodness, and that my life was inexplicable apart from the truth and beauty of Christ? She replied immediately that if I said that, she would say that I was born again!

Do you hear what I am saying? No matter what I said to her, all the varieties of our experience of Christ had to come down to the only way of expressing it she considered authentic. I had to say I had been born again. Now, I deplore that attitude, not only because it is unscriptural but because it is unchristian. It is wrong not only in fact but in attitude, not only in truth but in spirit. If we can find acceptance for our experience of God in Christ only when we put it in the words "born again", then we lose the sense of God's coming to each of us down His own secret stair. We must conform our experience to words that cannot express it.

I remember a young woman who once asked me, "What does it mean to be a Christian?" I knew her, and the quality of her Christian faith and life, so I turned the question and asked her what she thought it meant. She began to tell me of her Christian pilgrimage, full of her love for God and her devotion to His service. It was the story of one who had made progress and found joy in the faith. When she had finished, I told her that she very obviously knew what it meant to be a Christian; why had she asked? She had asked because she lived with a group of Christians who made it clear to her that if she did not have a Christian experience similar to theirs, and if she did not express this experience in their vocabulary, she was not a Christian. No wonder she found this disconcerting!

Years ago William Stringfellow came to the University of Western Ontario and delivered a series of powerful and moving lectures on the nature of faith. As the series went on, he sensed a growing unrest and dissatisfaction among a few members of the group, until finally, in the last lecture, one young lady rose to her feet and asked him right out if he had been born again. He replied that he had already expressed the reality and nature of his faith in a dozen different ways. None of them, it seemed, would do. Then he went on to lament that our understanding of the work of the Spirit of God has become so narrow that if it cannot be compressed into a definition of two words it is not even recognized. And then he asked, "Do you not realize that words are the most primitive form of faith?"

Why is it that we allow words to blind us to what is going on in a person's life? God does not have only one way by which He touches the human spirit; as George MacDonald said, He comes down His own secret stair into the life of each individual. The important thing is not *how* He comes but *that* He comes. And Christians should be eager to recognize and celebrate the varieties of His coming:

My fancied ways why should'st Thou heed?
Thou com'st down thine own secret stair;
Com'st down to answer all my need,
Yea, every bygone prayer!

A group of Christian fundamentalists in California once wrote to Karl Barth, perhaps the greatest theologian of our time, and a great and humble man who died only a few years ago. They enclosed a questionnaire and told him that they would like him to fill out the answers so that they could be sure that his faith was "sound." He replied by pointing out to them that the answers to all their questions were readily available in the books he had written and which they had not bothered to read. They had made no attempt to study his work or to understand his theology. Whatever he said to them they would interpret to suit themselves, and so he would give them neither a gentle nor an angry answer. He would give them no answer at all.

There is not one experience of the love of God in Christ; there are many. To be born again is one way of expressing that experience, but it is not the only way. It ought not to be made the one test of authentic faith.

II. Notice, next, that if I reply "yes" when asked if I am born again, I am declaring not only that I am a Christian, but that I am a Christian of a particular sort; for a born-again Christian is often one who has a very conservative theology, holds a literalist view of the inspiration of Scripture, and represents a cluster of ideas, theological, political, social and moral. Even if I am born again, I may not hold those views. To say "yes" then, is misleading.

Many born-again Christians, for example, make up what has come to be known as "The Moral Majority." Now, with some of the opinions of the Moral Majority, I have some sympathy; but not with all of their opinions, so I have no wish to be identified with them. Yet that is how some would think of me if I were to say I am a born-again Christian. If I were to say so, I should be doing much more than giving a formal testimony to the redeeming love of Christ; I should be making a theological, political, social and moral statement which I have no wish to make.

Further, many born-again Christians believe in eternal punishment, that those who are not born again will be eternally lost. I have heard this message from some of the television evangelists until I am sick of the sound of it. They believe that God will keep alive for ever those who have not been born again, so that He may eternally punish them for not being Christian. Such a view is immoral. No sin on earth, however heinous, can deserve torment of that sort. The distress loses all relation to the wickedness done, however dreadful it may have been. And the suffering is pointless. The damned cannot profit from it and the blessed are not edified by it. Yet it goes on senselessly and endlessly in an anguish of such dimensions as to outrage any conscience not impoverished by lack of imagination and distorted by the authority of a wrong-headed theology.

Some of you need to hear this because you sometimes try to make this church something which it is not. You hear that we are evangelical, that we preach the Gospel of God's grace. Of course we do. What else is there to preach? Attracted by this, you begin to attend, and then may find that we do not match all your expectations. You begin to think that we are not evangelical enough. It would please some of you if we were Bible literalists. But we are not. This church declares that one can be truly evangelical and at the same time bring to our understanding of Scripture the best insights of responsible modern scholarship. We welcome such scholars to our pews every Sunday. If being a born-again Christian has made you a Bible literalist or a theological fundamentalist, you will not be comfortable in this church. It might be better, then, both for you and for us, if you were to find a church closer to what you believe and wish to affirm. This church stands clearly for a particular point of view, and holds it with much love for those who disagree with us. But it is foolish, and leads to disappointment and regret, to try to make us what we are not.

III. Here is a third objection: Sometimes those who are born again make others feel inferior and convey to them a sense that they are not quite Christians. They sometimes have an air of smugness and condescension about them which hurts their cause and alienates many good people. Yet such an unhappy attitude is impossible once we understand what it means to be born again.

The Greek words for "born again" may be taken to mean one of two things, either "born again" or "born from above." But the Aramaic words that lie behind the Greek words *cannot* be translated "born again"; they can only be translated "born from above." Now the difference in meaning is not significant, but the difference in emphasis is crucial. If we are born from above it is not anything to be proud of because it is not anything that we have done. We are born "from above." I like that, because it puts the emphasis where it ought to be. If we are born from above, it is not our work but God's. And if that is true, then the experience is not a reason for conceit and arrogance, but for humility and praise. What is there to be proud of, and what is there in it to make us feel superior to others, when the work is God's and we are but the recipients of His grace? Sometimes a man who finds himself loved by a good woman will marvel, as the poet does, at the love he has encountered, and will ask with wondering joy, "Why, why and why?" That ought to be the normal attitude of faith. Dwelling in the love God has for us and the mercy that has redeemed us, we ask, "Why, why and why?"

IV. Here is the last objection. I abhor the fact that so many born-again Christians divide people into two groups. They separate them into the sheep and the goats, the right and the wrong, the born again and those who are not born again. They know exactly who is a Christian and who is not. I confess with the Psalmist that "such knowledge is too wonderful for me. It is high, I cannot attain unto it."

I received a letter once from an evangelical group at the University inviting me to speak there and pointing out with great care that I would be talking to "Christians and potential Christians." The person who wrote the letter obviously knew the difference, and who was Christian and who was "potential." I wondered how he knew. Do you think of people in that way? I do not think of people as "Christians and potential Christians." Do you think that when Jesus thought of people He placed them in those categories?

I have no sense of His doing so in the Gospels. He never lumped people together into one group labelled "sinners" and another called "the righteous." Each person He met was unique, with his own face, or her own form, and with needs, longings, failings, yearnings, peculiar to each one. And however close to God or far away from Him they thought themselves to be, they had all of our Lord's love and attention for He cared for them in themselves. He simply loved people and scorned the divisions and categories others imposed on them.

The parable of the great judgment is all about that. Those who thought they were saved, who *knew* they were saved, discovered that the saved are not always those who think they are. And those who were gathered into the joy of the Kingdom were astonished. They thought someone must have made a mistake! Whatever else the parable does, it rebukes our easy confidence that we know who is a Christian and who is not. Why are we so eager to divide people and to relish the thought of others being left out while we are gathered in? Is it not more fitting to remember that we are saved by grace, and that because we are, the difference between a good man and a bad man is insignificant in God's eyes. None of us is so good as not to stand in need of mercy, and none of us is so evil as to be beyond the reach of it.

Having said all that, let me now go on to say that we have a great deal to learn from many born-again Christians.

For one thing, they have a personal testimony to give. They have discovered a vital religion which they want to share. They know that they have moved from darkness to light, that their lives have been touched and transformed, that they live in a world loved by God and filled with Christ. They know Him and love Him and seek to serve Him. He is their own personal Saviour, and while that testimony does not and should not mark the outer limits of faith, it is a *very* good place for it to begin!

Harvey Cox once went and lived with people who had

turned from Western to Eastern religion. He wanted to understand why they had done so. Many of them had been Angli-
cans; some of them had been Presbyterians or Methodists or
Roman Catholics or Jews. They had been brought up in their
own faith, most of them. But Harvey Cox found that many of
them had grown weary of a faith that appeared to be all form
and no substance, with structures but little reality, with words
few of which ever touched their heart or quickened their spirit.
They said it was all second-hand, a conversation about something that happened to somebody else, an experience that
never became real. It was like reading the contents of the can
instead of being nourished by eating what was in it.

Now let me ask you: Is that a fair description of your faith?
I'm not asking you whether or not you are born again; I'm asking whether or not you know, live in and joyously return the
love God has for you. Have you allowed the grace of our Lord
Jesus Christ to move you from fear, hostility, estrangement, to
love, trust and joy in God? If, as the old Rabbis often asked
their pupils, you were asked to give the substance of your faith
while standing on one leg, what would you say? Would you
have anything to say worth saying?

Moreover, born-again Christians witness to the reality of a
conversion experience that can happen in a moment. They are
right about this. The New Testament is full of it. So is Christian history. Their united testimony is that a person's life can
be turned about in an instant. It happened to Saul of Tarsus
on the Road to Damascus, and to St. Augustine reading the
Scriptures in a garden. It happened to John Wesley when he
felt his heart strangely warmed and to C. S. Lewis riding on a
bus. Lewis went out on his journey an unbeliever in trouble,
and came home a Christian.

In our churches we stress the importance of Christian nurture. And so we ought. Some people have the idea that children belong to the devil and have to be won for God. We do
not believe that. We believe, with our Lord, that little children
already belong to God. They are His. He tells us that the Kingdom of God belongs to them. And the work of Christian nurture is to teach them to know and love and serve God faith-

fully and joyously. We want them to grow up in the warmth of God's love as naturally as flowers grow and blossom in His good sunshine.

But we must not forget that there are moments in everyone's life that make all moments. There are flashes of insight, times of crisis, glimpses of reality, intimations which make of life a whole new thing. The moments are not totally isolated from all others. It is as impossible to separate one moment in our life from those that have gone before and come up behind as it is to separate one wave of the sea from those that run ahead and those that follow after. Yet whatever leads to it, or flows from it, it is "God's moment" — the critical one which has the power to change all other moments forever. Falling in love can be like that. Moments of discovery can be like that. And falling in love with Jesus can be like that, and the discovery of grace. Browning tells us that truth may be flashed out in one blow, "and Guido see one instant and be saved."

That the experience may happen in an instant does not deny the place and value of Christian nurture. Paul had his moment of conversion on the road to Damascus, but he had seen Stephen stoned to death and had been haunted by it. John Wesley felt his heart strangely warmed in Aldersgate Street, but he had lived a life of Christian discipline and devotion. St. Augustine had his moment of revelation in the garden, but St. Augustine's mother had been praying for him for years, and he knew it. So let us say this for born-again Christians, that they hold to the reality that in any moment the Spirit of God may work in our life in such a way as to claim and transform it. Born-again Christians are quite sure of this, for they have experienced it.

Finally, one thing I love about born-again Christians is that they call themselves evangelical. Do you know what the word means? It means a declarer of good news. Born-again Christians declare the good news that God loves us so much that He gave His Son to reconcile us to Himself.

Let me remind you that the Gospel is good news and tell you that I would not be in this pulpit for two minutes if I did not have good news to declare. The Gospel is not a moral code. It is not social activism, though all manner of goodness flows from it, and it finds its expression in a care for all who are afflicted. It is good news about God's nature and what He has done on our behalf.

The Gospel is good news shouted in the street. You know the kind of news you can't wait to tell, and can't tell in a whisper. "She is graduating on Tuesday!" "Mary has taken a turn for the better!" "Charlie passed his examination!" "She is out of danger!" "Fred is coming home!" "Susan is getting married!" If I didn't feel like that about preaching the faith, I would not be a minister at all. What else is there to do, what else is there to declare? And this is the good news we declare: God loves you; He knows and calls you by name; He loves you personally, unconditionally, uniquely, eternally; He desires that you should love Him in return, for that would be your blessedness and fulfillment; He longs that you should trust Him as a little child trusts his father and mother and rejoices in the security and goodness of their love. That is what He wants. That is why Jesus came. And I do not care how it is expressed so long as the reality is possessed.

So let us be generous with one another, making room in our minds and hearts for those whose experience of Christ may not be like ours, but is authentic nonetheless. As Wesley loved to say, "If thy heart be as my heart, then give me thine hand."

THE JUDGMENT OF JUDGING

St. Mark 11:27–33

I am fascinated by the frequent encounters between our Lord and the chief priests, lawyers and elders who confronted Him demanding, "Tell us clearly who you are! Make it plain to us! Give us a sign! Tell us by what authority you do the things you do!" Time and time again they engaged Him, and as often as they asked, He answered. But His answers, at least to them, and perhaps to us, were not satisfactory. They seemed evasive. "Give us a sign!" they asked, and He replied that it is an evil generation that seeks a sign. No sign would be given. "Tell us who you are!" they demanded, and He replied that He *had* told them. "By what authority do you act?" they wanted to know. And he answered them with a question of His own about the authority of John the Baptist.

What is going on? Is Jesus just being difficult? Is He obstinate and perverse in refusing to give them a clear answer? Why does He not come right out and tell them what they want to know?

Our Lord was not being evasive, or perverse, or obstinate. His difficulty was that the answer to all their questions was in front of the eyes of anyone who had eyes to see. For example, they asked for a sign. But what sign could He give them? They already had the best and clearest sign. The truth is that He was Himself the sign, and if they could not find what they were looking for in Him they wouldn't see it in any other sign He might give them. "Show us clearly! Tell us plainly!" they demanded. He answered that He had shown them already and had told them plainly and they still couldn't or wouldn't see or hear. What was there left for Him to do? Was He simply to keep on repeating Himself, saying the same thing over and over again? But what help would that be? It was all there for them, but they had eyes and wouldn't see, and ears but wouldn't hear. Do you get a sense of our Lord's helplessness? What more could He do or say?

Others have experienced that sense of helplessness. Someone once asked Robert Frost, "Mr. Frost, what does that poem mean?" He replied, "What is it that you want me to do, say it again only worse?" Someone asked Pavlova, "What does that dance mean?" and she replied, "If I could have told you, I wouldn't have danced it!"

Now with Robert Frost it is, I suppose, intelligence that is called for to understand his poem, and we are not all brilliant. I find some of his poems difficult. I am not sure I understand them. With Pavlova, I suppose what was required to understand her work was a refined aesthetic sense, some appreciation of the art of the ballet. And some of us don't have a great deal of that. But not with our Lord! It wasn't brilliance that was needed to understand who He was and what He did. Their failure was not one of intellect but of attitude. Their *attitude* was wrong.

The common people knew where His authority came from. We read that "they were astonished at His teaching, for unlike their own teachers, He taught with a note of authority." *They* could see. *They* understood. *They* rightly interpreted the sign. *They* knew that His authority was something He carried with Him, in His own Person, and that it rested in the power of His truth to enlighten and persuade.

Not so with those who came demanding that He display His credentials! They couldn't or wouldn't see because their attitude was wrong. They didn't understand that their failure to see had more to do with their lack of perceptiveness than with His powers of demonstration.

Indeed, it would seem to me as I study the record, that there was one particular element in their attitude which by its very nature proved an almost impenetrable barrier to His appeal and rendered them incapable of seeing and hearing. It was that they saw themselves as His judges. They made Him somehow accountable to them. When they assumed that He was there to be judged and that they would do the judging; when they came at Him with an imperious demand, "Show us! Tell us! Prove your credentials!"; then the very conceit of their assumptions made it hard for them to see and hard for Him to show them.

What did our Lord do about it? He backed them off, that's what He did. He said, "You have been questioning me, now I am going to question you." Those who thought themselves His judges suddenly found themselves judged; those who had been asking questions were now questioned; and all this in the faint hope that they might begin to see that things were not the way they thought they were and that their attitude distorted their vision. I wonder if this was in our Lord's mind when on another occasion He said, "Judge not that you be not judged." Suddenly they found that their judgment was under judgment; that their stance, seemingly so dominant and confident, was precarious and false.

Of course the falseness of their attitude makes us question the appropriateness and integrity of our own. Have we eyes to see and ears to hear? Are we as blind and deaf to Him as they were? And for the same reason? How can we test our perception and clear our vision?

I.   *First of all, let us understand that we are judged.*

Do you ever scrutinize your own spiritual experience to find those points at which you are vulnerable? When I do so I find that I am threatened and uneasy when I am in the right. Not when I am in the wrong; being in the wrong brings its own chastening and imposes its own reticence. There is no temptation to arrogance when we know we are in the wrong. But when we are in the right we must be careful, for it is spiritually hazardous.

I was in the right once, and my being in the right meant that the other man, my adversary, was in the wrong. I knew it and he knew it. I had him just where I wanted him, and I loved it. I loved the power and moral superiority of it. And I hated myself for loving it. Thank God for the inner voice that whispered to me in the first flush of conceit, "Nobody, but nobody, is *that* right!"

The other times I find morally and spiritually threatening are when I sit in judgment. It is heady stuff, this judging of others. The power of it! The temptation to arrogance that is in it! It is so easy to be carried away by the whole thing and adopt an attitude of moral superiority, assuming that everything that is to be judged is out there in front of us, and that all the judgment is our own. What is there to see, then, but the mote in our brother's eye? Except that Jesus reminds us of the beam, the plank, that is in our own, so that our vision is distorted and we cannot see clearly to judge truly. It is not only the splinter in our brother's eye that calls for judgment, but the plank in our own. Judgment is not merely of the things we see, but of the way we see. In all our judgments we must be aware that we are judged.

Von Schlegel wrote a play in which the curtain rises to show an audience waiting for the curtain to go up. When it goes up it shows an audience waiting for the curtain to go up. The same thing happens again, and by this time the original audience, the real one, is feeling restless and uneasy. Are they, too, being watched?

Gogol wrote a play in which he revealed the emptiness of our pretensions and the foolishness of our hypocrisy. He mocks both, and has the audience laughing at those who are guilty of them. But suddenly, in the midst of the play, one of the characters faces the audience and asks who it is they are laughing at. He goes on to answer his own question. They are laughing at themselves, for nothing is revealed on the stage that is not present in the hearts of the audience.

Kierkegaard reminds us that when we come to worship there are no spectators. We are not permitted to come merely to watch and judge, for in worship there is only one Spectator and one Judge. He goes on to make fun of the way we talk about God in our ordinary conversations as though He were absent. He reminds us that all our comments, all our opinions, all our judgments of the divine ordering of things are spoken in the divine Presence. Do you know what he is saying to us? That when we are judging, what is to be judged is not out there in front of us. We are in the picture; we had better look over our shoulder because in our judging we are judged.

II. *Notice, not only that we are judged, but that we are judged by our judgments.*

Sometimes we are condemned by them. We are judged by them because they reveal us, give us away. They declare our insight, or lack of it; our intelligence or lack of it; our sensitivity, or lack of it. Our values, our perceptiveness, our wisdom are all revealed when we judge. So we must be very careful, knowing that every opinion we express tells something about us.

Did you hear of the woman who was being shown through an art gallery and who moved from room to room and from picture to picture commenting, "I don't see much in that!"? The attendant who accompanied the group listened to her until he could stand it no longer; quietly he told her, "Madam, the pictures are not on trial."

There is a wonderful story told of Joseph Parker of London's City Temple, and a prince of preachers. One Sunday morning Parker told his huge congregation that before the service someone had written him an intimidating note and slipped it under his study door. It informed him that the writer would be present at worship and intended to make a critical assessment of the sermon, a philosophical analysis of every sentence the preacher uttered. Parker went on to say that at first reading the note filled him with dismay. Who could stand such scrutiny? He had taken the trouble to read it twice, however, and lost most of his trepidation when he noticed that the writer spelled "philosophical" with an "f."

Gilbert Frankau's mother used to put on cultural and social occasions nearly every Sunday evening. She would invite artists to come and sing and play for her guests. One evening she invited a young Australian soprano to come and sing. When it was over she wrote a comment about the singer in her diary. "What an appalling voice," she wrote, "the woman ought to be muzzled and never allowed to sing again." The young soprano was Nellie Melba.

Here is a literary critic writing in the *Edinburgh Review* and declaring adamantly, "The poem simply will not do!" The poem that "would not do" was William Wordsworth's "The Excursion."

"Judge not that you be not judged," says our Lord, because He knows that our judgments give us away. We think we are doing the judging, but the very words we speak are the words that judge us. This can be lightsome and humorous, as we have seen. It can also be tragic. Herod, Pilate, Caiaphas, all in the conceit and arrogance of power, judged Jesus. And Herod, Pilate and Caiaphas have been condemned by their judgment ever since.

Haven't you noticed that our judgment of other people's character reveals our own? We listen to those who are critical of the gifts and accomplishments of others, and say to ourselves, "Why are they so bitter, or jealous, or resentful?" Their criticism reveals more of themselves than of those whom they criticize. Their insecurity, their inferiority, their envy, shows in their criticism so that we want to tell them, "Don't say another word! Every word you speak gives you away!" We are judged, and our judgments judge us. Sometimes they condemn us.

III.   *Knowing that we are judged heightens our sense of responsibility.*

In this way it can do great things for our character, for it deepens our sense of being accountable. The turning point in The Book of Job comes when Job, who has made all his complaints against God, has asked all his questions, expressed all his impatience, given voice to all his dissatisfaction, is answered by God out of a whirlwind. And what is God's answer? It is to ask Job a question! Suddenly the questioner has not only asked a question, but must give an answer. And God's question of Job sets his complaint within the wonder of creation until he is made to realize, in the words of Thomas

Traherne, "how lately he was made and how wonderful it was when he came into it." The *details* of God's answer to Job are outside the scope of this sermon, but the *effect* of God's question on Job is immediate and compelling. Job is silenced and humbled and then moved to adoration when he cannot begin to answer the God he has so vigorously questioned.

Victor Frankel tells us that the difference between those who survived the appalling conditions in the Nazi concentration camp in which he was confined, and those who did not, had little to do with their size or physical strength. The determining difference was that some thought they were asking the questions and others knew that they were being questioned. Some of them asked, "Why should this happen to me? What have I done to deserve this? Why has life done this to me?" Those who talked like that often sank into self-pity and lost the will to survive. But there were others who believed, not that they were to question life but that life was questioning them. Their awareness of being tested, and the sense of accountability it created, strengthened them to come through. The difference between life and death was whether they saw themselves as the questioners or the questioned. Those who survived were convinced that the most important thing in life is not what happens to us, but what we do with what happens to us.

I read once of a young girl, raised in rural America in times when there were seven grades in one school, of one room, with one teacher. One day she complained to her mother of her lack of opportunity. Her mother, of pioneering stock and spirit, replied, "Don't complain to me about that! I have given you life and being; I may not be able to give you much more, but I have given you that, and it is up to you to do what you can with it." That "hard" word was a saving word. It stopped the girl from feeling sorry for herself, deepened her sense of personal responsibility and strengthened her will. She went on to make the most of her opportunity, limited as it was, and became a distinguished scholar in her own right and the wife of a university president. The change came about when she realized that life was not on trial; she was. She was not asking the questions; life was.

It can be like that with us in a matter as elevated as our sense of moral indignation. We rage, and rightly so, against the predicament of the homeless in our city, or of the hungry in our world, or the victims of war or revolution. Our hearts go out especially to little children. We ask why God allows so much suffering and why He appears to do so little to redress the injustices of our world. We echo old Thomas Carlyle's complaint, "God sits in heaven and does nothing!" Yet often our moral indignation is not matched by our Christian compassion. We'd rather ask God the question than acknowledge that we are part of the answer. We forget that God's loving intention for His world calls us to be the instruments of His good purpose. If we allow our moral indignation to ask God the question, we must not be surprised when God's answer is to ask us what we are doing about the injustices that kindle our indignation. We often have it within our power to right the very wrongs which make us question God's goodness! We are not only the askers of the question; we are required to answer.

IV. *Finally, we are judged because our judgments have consequences.*

We sometimes judge others, express our criticism of them to them, and think it ends there. We imagine that the matter rests where we left it. We seldom stop to think that what we say has an effect. Our judgments, our verdicts, especially if they are harsh judgments of other people, do make a difference to the way they feel, the way they think, and ultimately to what they will do in response or reaction to our words. We judge them; but they will judge our judgments, and will decide how to deal with them and with us. So we must be careful, for our judgments do have consequences. Sometimes we call these consequences the wrath of God, or "fearful symmetry" as Blake called them, or dramatic irony. It doesn't matter what we call the consequences, so long as we believe the reality of them. Sooner or later our judgments judge us. We are judged by their consequences.

This holds true, not only of what we say to other people or

the way we treat them, but of what we do to ourselves. All the
time, we are making judgments about our life, its goals and
values, what we are after, what is of first importance to us. How
shall we decide? Is it money, or power, or sex, or fame that
we're after? We make our decision about that, but it doesn't
end there. As surely as you are sitting in this church, that judgment will be judged, for it will have consequences, and they
will be to our joy or sorrow, our fulfillment or emptiness, for
we have no right to expect more than our chosen values can
deliver. Does that sound difficult? Let me make it plain.

If you put self at the center, you must be prepared to find
your outer limits there, and that can be very lonely. If what you
are after is power, you had better forget about affection, for it is
very difficult to have both. If you really think that life is a rat-
race, you must not look for any dignity in it. If you have made
up your mind that life is purely quantitative, then you had better keep your averages up. If you are a gossip, you mustn't
expect confidences. If it is your practice to confront people,
then don't expect them to come knocking on your door when
what they need is tenderness. If what you are really after is
security, you had better forget about ecstasy. If you think your
children are among your own private possessions, then you
must not look for creative and spontaneous spirits. If you
really are a materialist, then don't consult us gurus about spiritual values for there is very little we have to say to you, and
even less that you would understand. If you are possessed by
your profession, you had better keep one eye on your relationships. If you are interested only in justice and not in mercy,
you'd better not make any mistakes. If you are unscrupulously
ambitious, you must not expect trustful friends. And if you
decide to live by the sword, then by God you had better carry
one. Do you know why? Because life is moral, that's why;
because our judgments really do come back to us for good or
ill; we really do, in the end, reap what we sow and not any
more; and the chickens really do come home to roost.

"Show us clearly! Tell us plainly! Who are you? Give us a
sign! By what authority?" we demand, in questions that are
sometimes distorted by arrogance and blinded by conceit. And

all the time it would be far more fitting if we were to utter a prayer born of our weakness and shaped by our infirmity: "Lord, that we might receive our sight!"

COME OUT THE WILDERNESS!

St. Matthew 4:1-11

I want to talk to you about the wilderness. One of the meanings of the Hebrew word for wilderness is "a place you pass through." I did that once, passing through the Judean Wilderness in an air-conditioned Mercedes-Benz bus. If you're going to pass through the wilderness, that's the way to do it. I passed through it. Bishop James Pike of New York City did not. He and his wife parked their car at the side of the wilderness road and wandered a little way into the desert. They couldn't find their way back. Bishop Pike perished in the wilderness, and his wife nearly did. A wilderness is a place you pass through. If you don't pass through it you will perish in it.

Notice that we speak of the "wilderness" not only as a geographical location, but as a region of the human spirit and a dimension of human experience. And my message to you is very simple. I can put it in one sentence: A wilderness experience is one you pass through.

But before we develop that point, here is a preliminary truth to notice:

I. *Some people* make *life a wilderness by the way they pass through it.*

They pay little attention to it; they are not moved to wonder by its beauty, nor to gratitude by its generosity, nor to humour by its pretensions, nor to reverence by its grandeur, nor to pity by its tragedy. They do not allow themselves to perceive, or celebrate it. Elizabeth Barrett Browning laments that every bush may be ablaze with God's glory, but we do not notice it, prefer-

76

ring to gather blackberries instead. We stand every day on holy ground, but are not aware of it. We take something beautiful and make it a wilderness simply by passing through it with never a perceptive look to left or right, and so miss its splendor. That is why Jesus said, "*Perceive* the lilies of the field"; that is, don't just look at them, *perceive* them. He lamented that so many have eyes but do not see, and ears but do not hear. He not only looked, but saw with the eyes of wonder. How sad if we should miss the many-splendored thing!

One of the most useful functions of prophets, saints, artists and scientists is that they help us to notice things. Someone remarked once that poets see more in an apple than many of us see in all the wonders that surround us, for in it they find the snows of winter and the blossom of spring and the "mists and mellow fruitfulness" of autumn. Thomas Hardy once remarked that he wished to be remembered as a poet who *noticed* things.

A woman came to the great J. M. W. Turner and complained that she never saw the sunsets Turner painted. The artist replied, "But madam, don't you wish you did?" I read recently of a young man who for the first time attended an orchestral concert. The music was an enchantment. How he hated to make "the journey homeward to habitual self." He turned to the person sitting beside him and asked with a kind of wonder, "How long has this been going on?" The answer is, of course, that it has been going on for a long time, for us as well as for him, and often the sweet sounds and noble melodies have fallen on deaf ears.

The mystics and poets can help us enormously here. Thomas Traherne reminds us that the sea itself can flow in our veins, the stars can be our crown, and that we can never enjoy the world alright until we delight in God's creation more than misers do in gold and kings in scepters. He tells us that we are dead to the splendor of God's creation until we remember "how lately we were made and how wonderful it was when we came into it."

How sad to be here and miss the glory in things! The Stoics were sometimes guilty of that. They wanted to be invulnerable, to keep control of their lives by a rational principle that ordered their days securely. They always guarded their feelings, afraid that if they loved anything or anyone too much they might be hurt by rejection or death. They would not allow themselves to become too attached to anything for fear that it might be taken away from them. The cost of such security, however, was any hope of ecstasy, and the kind of celebration Traherne exulted in passed them by. Someone remarked of them that "they made of life a desert and called it peace." They were a bit like a cheap sound system that can't pick up the highest notes and the lowest. Yet that is where much of the music is! They never descended into the depths of the human condition, and they never reached the heights of it either. Their lives did not *sing*.

Some Christians are like that. When I was growing up in the church, I used to hear an old chorus that declared, "Earth is but a desert drear, heaven is my home." Even then I sensed the ingratitude of the words. We may have wilderness experiences, but earth is not a desert drear, for it is God's handiwork. At its creation, "the morning stars sang together and all the sons of God shouted for joy," and God looked at it and pronounced, "it is very good!"

I wonder if God does not think us ungrateful when we receive His good gifts with so little joy. One of my old college professors used to remind his students often that "on the Day of Judgment we shall be called to account, not only for those sins we have committed, but for those good gifts of God we have not enjoyed." All Puritans were not like the one described in this little poem, but some of them were:

> The puritan through life's sweet garden goes,
> And plucks the thorn and throws away the rose.
> He thinks to please by this peculiar whim,
> The God who made and fashioned it for him.

Surely Christians ought to enjoy the world not less, but more than worldly people, for to all other qualities is added the awareness that all loveliness is God's good gift and that He has given us "all good things richly to enjoy." We should celebrate the work of the Creative Spirit more than unbelievers, because we believe it is *His* Spirit. Loving our dear ones, we rejoice that we are sharing in God's love for all that He has made. It is in the mystery, grandeur and majesty of the stars and mountains and oceans that we find the very vocabulary in which to express the majesty and eternity of God. Your sweetheart is not just yours, she is God's as well, and He loves her even more than you do! You just share the love that created her and made her the wonder that she is! And the music you listen to! Did you ever think that to make it, God had to make the musicians who composed it? We have *King Lear* only because God made Shakespeare. How sad that one of the followers of John Wesley burned his master's annotated Shakespeare, thinking that an interest in drama was not fitting for a holy man! How I wish we could have had Wesley's insights and perceptions, for his was a well-furnished mind, and he was an astute critic.

Don't make the world a desert by passing through it with blind eyes and deaf ears! To do so is to have part in that ingratitude which Karl Barth tells us is the root of all sin. Take this world of wonders from God's hand and celebrate it joyously, deeply, responsibly, and offer it back to Him in praise and thanksgiving.

II.   *It is enormously strengthening to remember that the wilderness experiences we pass through will pass.*

For years I have been sustained by the words of Nathaniel Hawthorne that "the greatest of all mortal consolations is that this, too, will pass." Sometimes, then, in our distress, it is comforting to remember that all we need is time. We should know that. When we have a cold we deplore the inconvenience of it but know that in five or six days it will be over. A cut on our finger makes it awkward to handle things, but we know that in a few days it will heal. When we have been emotionally wounded by disappointment, humiliation or sorrow, we know that the greatest anguish is at the beginning, and that time will heal, or at least afford other influences an opportunity to heal us. Experience tells us that it is so. Do you remember the occasion when you were deeply hurt by the unkindness of someone you loved? The shock of it was appalling; you couldn't understand it. But as the days passed you gathered it into yourself and in some sense came to terms with it. It still hurts, and it still perplexes you why it should have happened, but the pain is not as sharp as it once was, and it no longer drains you of most of your emotional energy.

Singers and actors know that when they have performed poorly they feel diminished. The week that follows a Sunday on which I feel I haven't preached well is a difficult six days, but it brings another Sunday and there is a faithful congregation waiting with a sense of expectancy and affording me a fresh opportunity to preach. The next performance brings a new opportunity to singers and actors to do it again and better, and so they wait patiently for it. Experienced ball-players who go into a slump and can't hit or catch or pitch or throw know that it won't last for ever. They've been through it before and have come out of it.

Dr. Leslie Weatherhead was not only one of the world's great preachers, he was a distinguished psychologist. In middle-age he entered a period of depression that was one of almost unrelieved darkness. One of the things that helped him most was a quotation from Browning's *Paracelsus*:

> If I stoop into a dark tremendous sea of cloud
>   It is but for a time.
> I hold God's lamp close to my breast.
> Its splendor soon or late will pierce the gloom.
>   I shall emerge one day.

In the darkest night of his life the sentence that he held on to, and which helped to bring him through, was "I shall emerge one day." Many of the wilderness experiences we must pass through will themselves pass away. And so our waiting has a quality of hopefulness about it. Often we become impatient when we have to wait, and it is easy to think that waiting is characterized by fretfulness. But deeper than our fretfulness and impatience is hope. We know that sooner or later the waiting will be over and what we wait for will be gained. If there is no sense of expectancy about our waiting, then it is no longer waiting, it is despair.

I met a woman once who had come through frequent periods of depression. I asked her, "How are you?" She replied, with a serenity gained from long experience, "I'm waiting." She had stooped again into that "dark tremendous sea of cloud" which she knew so well; but she knew also that with help from her physician and her friends she would get the days in and, in a little while, would emerge.

Listen! Sometimes it is victory in itself just to get the days in. We are sometimes disappointed that in our difficult times we are not splendidly heroic and grandly triumphant. We should realize that sometimes it takes all the courage we have just to get the days in. We must tell ourselves clearly, for our strengthening, that waiting is a kind of doing. Sometimes just to get the days in is all the victory we should expect; to get through the difficult hours and not give in or give up is an important victory in itself. It is like a boxer who has been hit with a heavy punch. All he can do is hold on to the end of the round. There is no glory in holding on, and not much dignity either; but it is not a matter of glory, it is a matter of survival. So he throws his arms around his opponent and tries to get through what remains of the three-minute round. Then he will have a minute's respite in which to recover his strength and go on.

The knowledge that waiting is a kind of doing might well have been learned from the Irish and their wise use of their round towers. A round tower looks a bit like a pencil set on end with its point towards the sky. It has a door, reached by a ladder, about a third of the way up. When attacked by raiders (mostly the Scots) the Irish would enter the door, pull the ladder up inside the tower, shut the door, and wait in the well-provisioned tower for their enemies to go home. Sometimes they shouted rude words at them in gaelic which is a wonderful language for swearing. They just waited out the necessary time.

They got the days in without surrender and emerged to get on with their life.

What kind of wilderness experience are you passing through? Some of you are worried about your business, others about your relationships, or your health, or your children. It is so easy when we are emotionally spent to believe that things will remain forever in the same unhappy state they are in now. But often that is not the case. Often the wilderness experience through which we must pass will itself pass. That is one of our consolations, and it is a very great one.

III.   *Passing experiences may yield lasting benefits.*

This is especially true of our wilderness experiences. They caused us great distress; we should not wish to go through them again; indeed, we should not wish them upon anyone. Yet, in retrospect, painful as they were, they deepened us in ways that awaken our gratitude. The truth of this was expressed in one sentence by an old sailor who had often sailed in turbulent waters: "I do not like being in a storm at sea, but I like having been in a storm at sea." Someone who was long in a wilderness of suffering emerged, and honored the richness that was found there by saying that while suffering passes, to have suffered never passes.

That is one of the reasons why we like to remember the difficult times in our lives. With old friends we talk about the old days when we struggled to provide food and shelter, or to gain an education, or to build a business. We remember the sense of desperation we felt, the despair when things looked hopeless, the temptation to self-pity that threatened us. But we came through, and the mark of those days is on us still, for we knew we were alive and we felt the grain of existence and the stirrings in us of a courage and determination we never knew we had and, indeed, did not have until they were required of us. Those qualities endure, for they are part of our sense of self forever. That is why Winston Churchill's words to England under attack struck deep in every heart, and challenge us still. He exhorted his people to brace themselves with such courage and tenacity that the wilderness hours would be remembered not only as their darkest hours but as their finest.

Once we give it our attention, it is easy to understand why the wilderness experiences we pass through can bring us permanent benefit. It is because so many of the qualities we covet for ourselves can be won only through adversity. There is no other way to have them but to find them in demanding and difficult circumstances.

That is why we must be careful what we pray for. Sometimes the qualities we ask God to give us can be received only in circumstances not pleasing to us. Suppose, for example, we were to ask God for courage. How are we to have it except by passing through experiences that demand it? But such experiences are not pleasant, for courage is always difficult. There is no such thing as easy courage. We ask for courage, but are we ready to face the difficulties that are the condition of our having it?

Here is a man who, impatient with his own lack of patience, asked God for the gift of it. The next morning he missed his train and had to spend an hour, restless and fretful, waiting for the next one. Until he suddenly realized that if he wished to learn to be patient he would have to do so in circumstances in which it would be much easier to be impatient — such as having to wait an hour for a train! He hadn't thought of that when he asked God for patience!

Do you remember Hemingway's fine definition of fortitude? He called it "grace under pressure." But that means that if you seek the grace of fortitude you had better be prepared for the pressure. Again, we may ask God to increase our hope, that we may be saved from despair. But how can we gain hope except in circumstances so distressing as to tempt us to hopelessness? Such circumstances are not really anything we would wish for, yet they yield a lasting enrichment. Listen:

> I walked a mile with pleasure.
> She chattered all the way,
> But left me none the wiser
> For all she had to say.

I walked a mile with sorrow,
And never a word said she,
But Oh! the things I learned from her
When sorrow walked with me!

Such qualities as those we have mentioned are not ours, and cannot be ours, simply by our asking. They carry their cost with them, and often lead us through the wilderness before we find them.

That gives me a clue to a strange verse which introduces our Lord's temptations: "Then was Jesus led by the Spirit into the wilderness to be tempted of the Devil." Do you perceive the oddness of the words? Why does the *Spirit* lead Him into the wilderness to face the Devil's testing? It is to teach us that while temptation is the Devil's work, it is the Spirit who brings us to and through the wilderness experience of temptation and so strengthens our character forever. It is in this sense that we understand and affirm the powerful words of Unamuno with which he closes his book *The Tragic Sense of Life*:

May God deny you Peace
That He may give you Glory!

Wilderness experiences are to be passed through. If we abide in them, we shall perish in them. If we allow ourselves to linger or to dwell in them, they will destroy us. Our choice is to stay in the desert and perish or pass through it and possess forever the graces we find there. Always the temptation is to regard as a settled state the wilderness experience which is but a stage in our pilgrimage. In this sermon and the two to follow, I want to identify some such experiences.

1.   *We must pass through guilt to forgiveness.*

Guilt is something to be passed through. Some Christians do not think so. They believe not only that it is a permanent state of the spiritual life, but that it ought to be. They would tell us that the only good conscience is a bad conscience, and that the normal condition of the Christian life is a sense of sin.

I want to affirm with all the power I possess that the normal condition of the Christian life is not a sense of sin but the reality of grace. We are *not* sinners. We are *forgiven* sinners, and that word is the difference between dying in the desert and dwelling in the promised land. Guilt is not something in which we dwell, but something through which we pass. It is left behind as we enter the realm of God's grace. The Scriptures express this with great beauty when they say that God has *forgotten* our sin. Nothing is more perfectly left behind than something that has been faced and then forgotten. Surely when the completeness of God's forgiveness of us is so clearly stated, we ought to believe it ourselves and stop dwelling in our guilt. As one of the great and wise saints of the church used to say, "What God has forgotten, 'tis no business of ours to remember." I love to think of how Paul Tillich describes forgiveness when he tells us that it is the past that is remembered that it may be forgotten.

It follows, then, that the normal condition of the Christian life is the enjoyment of a good conscience, not the tyranny of a bad one. This must be so when we consider the nature of conscience. What is it but an appetite for moral truth that enables us to discern what is good that we may embrace it and to recognize what is evil that we may turn from it? It commends us when we do what is right and sounds an alarm when we are tempted to do wrong.

Now, it is not the function of an alarm to ring all the time. Its value is that it doesn't ring all the time, but only when it is necessary to sound an alarm and to take warning from it. How annoying when, as frequently happens, the anti-theft alarm goes off in a parked car and keeps on sounding. It can disturb a whole neighborhood for an hour. That it does so is not a sign of its usefulness, but a sign that it isn't working right. Similarly, you do not sound the horn on your car all the time (though New York cab-drivers do). Most people use it sparingly, only when it is needed to warn others of our presence. A friend of mine was driving in Toronto at rush hour when the horn of his car started to blare and wouldn't stop. This did not please him. It did not please the cars in front of him. By the time he arrived home he was in great distress caused by a horn that didn't know when to stop.

A good conscience is one that sounds an alarm and, having gained our attention and response, is happy to be silent until the next time it is needed. Its function is not to make us dwell in a sense of guilt, but to lead us from the distress of a bad conscience to the peace of a good one.

Once we truly believe that guilt is a wilderness experience to be passed through on the way to something better, every part of our Christian life will gain in confidence and joy. Our prayers, for example. So often we plead with God for forgiveness over and over again, so dwelling on our guilt and sin that we strengthen their hold on us. We should be wiser to plead less and affirm more confidently that God *has* forgiven us, that He delights to do so, that we live in a forgiven universe. Every prayer of confession should be followed by an assurance of pardon that declares we have received forgiveness for the sins we have confessed.

Let me close with words which express with enormous power and a most moving tenderness the completeness of God's forgiveness of us. Do you remember how, in *Pilgrim's Progress*, Christian passes along the Highway of Salvation to a hill called Calvary, at the foot of which there is a sepulchre and at the top of which there is a cross? He climbs slowly, for he carries a heavy burden of guilt upon his back:

> So I saw in my dream, that just as Christian came up with the cross, his burden loosed from his shoulders, and fell from off his back, and began to tumble, and so continued to do till it came to the mouth of the sepulchre, where it fell in, *and I saw it no more.*
>
> Then was Christian glad and lightsome, and said with a merry heart, 'He hath given me rest by His sorrow and life by His death.' Then he stood still awhile to look and wonder; for it was very surprising to him that the sign of the cross should thus ease him of his burden. He looked, therefore, and looked again, even till the springs that were in his head sent the water down his cheeks . . . Then Christian gave three leaps for joy, and went on, singing.

Come out the wilderness! Why would you wish to dwell there when there is a land of promise waiting for you, and One there who beckons you into it?

COME OUT THE WILDERNESS!
PART II

DEATH IN THE DESERT

St. Matthew 4:1-11

We noticed in an earlier sermon that a wilderness experience is one we pass through. We went on to say that we should pass through guilt to forgiveness.

Continuing our thought, here are more "wildernesses" to leave behind:

1. *We must get beyond justifying ourselves to expressing ourselves.*

Albert Camus once remarked that we hardly need to fear the judgment of God for it could not be more severe than the judgment of other people. Yet I sometimes think that the bitterest judgment of all is our judgment of ourselves. We accuse ourselves harshly and live in an atmosphere of self-condemnation.

Some of us do so because we are perfectionists, hardly pausing to think that if we have such unrealistically high expectations of ourselves we are sure to fail; and what is left then but self-rejection? Our failure to achieve one-hundred percent all the time makes the attempt to justify ourselves a full-time occupation. We feel we are never good enough however good we are; we never manage to please ourselves however hard we try. So we find no sense of peace, but feel the torment of having to justify ourselves to ourselves and others. Always we are a little less than we think we ought to be, and no perfectionist can bear it.

I know some good people who must be busy all the time, driven by a sense of urgency and desperation. They are driven, not because they feel they are doing important and useful things but because every day is one in which they must justify their existence. If they take a day off, they feel guilty about it. They tell themselves it is because they are devoted to their work, and there may well be truth in that; but it is not a joyous commitment, for it has too much strain in it. Sometimes, indeed, it is the expression of spiritual sickness, for it lacks the grace of self-acceptance. How else are we to make ourselves acceptable to God and others, and hold on to even a minimal self-regard, if we do not justify ourselves every instant? So the busyness of every moment is not a joyous expression of our interests, but a torment by which we seek to justify ourselves.

For some of us, it started with our parents. We thought their love was something we had to win, that it was ours only if we deserved it and so long as we deserved it. The trouble is that once we began to think like that, we never could believe that we had done enough to deserve their love. We had to keep on trying all the time.

I know husbands and wives who after years of marriage are still trying to earn each other's love, to deserve it and win their partner's approval. What an uphill road that is! It winds uphill all the way, to the very end. What a difference it makes when we know that we are loved, cherished, adored, before we have done anything to deserve it; when love is not something to be earned, but is freely given and joyously received; when we feel no need to justify ourselves or to make ourselves acceptable, because we are accepted already.

Young people, when they fall in love, or would like to fall in love, filled with all the hope and anxiety of it, imagine that they might be loved if they were different. So they try to earn the other's love, thinking they are not worthy to be loved just as they are. Young lady, if he will love you only if you are different, then find someone else. He isn't right for you. Young man, if she will love you only if you keep proving yourself, find someone else. She isn't right for you. True love is not offered to us on condition that we change; it cherishes and delights in us and tells us, "Stay as sweet as you are! Don't let a thing ever change you!" Surely the deepest joy is to be loved as we are and because of what we are.

We do it with God. Many of us believe that God's love is something we have to deserve, and therefore something which has to be earned. How are we to earn it? By good works? But then we are told that our good works are really not any good. So we try to do it by having faith, or by repentance. But that just makes faith and repentance another kind of good works. It seems that whatever we do fails to give us the answer we need, for all our efforts perish in the mistaken idea that the good will of God is something we must win, not something God already has for us. We even allow this idea to distort the Christian faith. We interpret the work of Jesus as His attempt to persuade God to love us. God is against us, and only His Son, having great influence with the Father, can persuade Him to be gracious to us. But how can we ever be sure that God loves us when He has to be *persuaded* to love us?

No wonder many of us have gone through most of our lives with a deep, though sometimes unrealized or unacknowledged, sense of grievance against God. Somebody said once that when we cannot have the good opinion of someone we come very near to hating them. And deep in many of us is a sense of resentment against God, or our parents, or our husband or wife, because we could not have their good opinion of us. We have never been sure that we've done enough to earn it. What we have is a sense of helplessness, often deepened by the kind of religion that tells us that there is nothing we can do to deserve God's love or earn it, for we have no goodness of our own to offer Him.

I'm sure you've noticed that this effort to justify ourselves takes so much energy and creates such a sense of defensiveness that it becomes difficult for us to express ourselves. It seems that we are always trying to make up lost ground, coming from behind, being scrutinized, assessed and found wanting. In such a deadly atmosphere, what personality can express itself freely and joyously? Those who are constantly critical of us will never know us. They say love is blind;

but love sees more than suspicion and contempt, for when we are loved it allows us to show ourselves without fear of rejection. The critical spirit is cold enough to chill the warmth of the most spontaneous and lightsome spirit. It is not that we *will* not reveal ourselves; we *cannot* reveal ourselves in such threatening circumstances. We are too busy keeping our defenses up, guarding our fragile good opinion of ourselves, holding on to whatever fragments of self-esteem we can retain. This takes all our attention and determines our mood.

How are we to deal with it? Let us begin by affirming that we do not need to justify ourselves, for we are already justified; we do not need to earn God's favour, or to deserve it, for He loves us already. We already have His good will. We live in what someone has called "a ceaseless flow of loving acceptance." Remember the phrase! Of course we are helpless and unable to earn God's love. How can we earn what is offered to us as a gift? Of course we cannot deserve God's favor, not because God is impossible to please, not because we have nothing to offer that would please Him, but because He loves us unconditionally before we have done anything to deserve it. This is a most happy helplessness! We are helpless as my children are helpless. There is nothing they can do to win my good will or earn my love. I should be horrified to think of their trying to. They can't earn my love because it is already theirs; it has surrounded them from their very beginning; they were *loved* into existence. Why should they seek to justify themselves when they know that I delight in them already and that to love them is the deepest joy of my life?

We sometimes forget that when Jesus taught us to think of God as our Father, He meant also that God thinks of us as His children. And what we wish for our children is not that they should dwell in the wilderness of trying to justify themselves to us, but that they should believe and live in the joy of the love we already bear them. God's love for us, like our love for them, was there at the beginning. It is something freely bestowed at the start, not something we have achieved at the end. It is one of life's ironies that we spend so much time trying to justify ourselves to God when all the time He is working by His gracious Spirit to persuade us of the great love He already bears us, and to win us from suspicion, grievance and fear to the glorious liberty of the children of God! The work of Jesus is not to persuade God to love us. Jesus is God's way of convincing us that He loves us enough to lay down His life for our sake.

The moment we believe this, our life will be changed for ever. We shall know that God does not love us because we have value but that we have value because we are so greatly loved. Instead of striving for a love that we want but cannot deserve, we shall dwell in a love that is ours already. We shall understand that Jesus is not on our side against God, but is God's way of showing us that God Himself is on our side and, indeed, never was against us. We are loved uniquely, unconditionally, eternally; and if that is the truth of the Gospel, then we shall delight God's heart by believing it and living in the joy and freedom of it. It is such love that brings us alive, enabling us to express all that is best in us:

> That Thou should'st think so much of me,
> And be the God Thou art,
> Is darkness to my intellect,
> But sunshine to my heart.

2. *We must move through doubt to faith.*

St. Paul says that we see through a glass darkly; that we discern only baffling reflections in a mirror; and because of that, we are often perplexed and uncertain. And that is not a bad thing. It belongs to the human condition. Plato was not far from St. Paul in his own great image of human knowledge as shadows cast by the flickering flames of a fire on the walls of the cave in which we dwell. We do not know everything, and we are not going to. We can be certain of only a few things. And this is true of our religion. I am not attracted by those Christians who have an easy answer to every question; I am repelled by them. They know, or think they know, all about God and so reduce the Eternal to the dimensions of their own mind. Their success is their punishment. If God is small enough to be held within the range of our thought of Him, He has ceased to be God. He can no longer be the center of our worship, for we have made Him smaller than we are. There is no room for doubt in such a faith, for we have purged it of its mystery. We have made faith impossible.

I should think that all true faith must have a large element of agnosticism in it. About many matters it is perfectly appropriate for the Christian to say, "I do not know." But this kind of uncertainty is not a barrier to faith, it is an element in it and an expression of it. Indeed, it is the cutting edge of faith and leads to its refinement and its strengthening. Unamuno, the great Spanish poet and philosopher, questioned whether faith could be faith if it lacked this quality of doubt. He would assert that faith lives by this sort of doubt, for doubt poses the questions and shapes them, and sets us searching for the truth that faith may discover.

I must tell you how strongly I agree with Unamuno. My faith and ministry owe far more to my skepticism than to my credulity. If I had not felt and faced my doubts, I should be of very little use to you. Few of your questions surprise me, for they have been my questions too. I have grown in faith by exchanging one lot of questions for another and deeper lot, and the resolving of them has been the joy and adventure of my pilgrimage. I can say with Dostoevsky, "My hosanna has come forth from the crucible of doubt."

All the great believers have been incredulous. The greatest believers have been the greatest doubters. Their restless, searching minds have questioned faith and won through to clearer insight and deeper understanding. Someone once described Alex Vidler as "the quintessential Anglican, who loves God with his whole heart and doubts Him with his whole mind!" Yet many of us were taught that to doubt was wicked, and we were instructed to put our doubts out of our minds. Having faith meant not having any doubts, so some gave up their doubts. Others, unhappily, give up their faith.

When young people bring their questions of faith to me, I do not tell them to put them out of their minds, but to regard them as the work of God's Spirit leading them into deeper truth. It was Jesus who told us that we should love God with our minds. The Spirit teaches us the best questions to ask, and gives us the insights that illumine them. To face the questions that arise for faith in this way seems to me to be obedience to Paul's exhortation that we should "work out our own salvation in fear and trembling, knowing that it is God who is working in us both to will and to do His good pleasure." When people come to me with the doubts that assail them, I often share with them the great words of Rainer Maria Rilke, "Be patient towards all that is unsolved in your heart, and learn to love the questions themselves." Young people, if you have no questions for faith, you are not thinking! This sort of questioning I never want to leave behind. It is a perpetual stimulation of my faith. I anticipate and hope that for the rest of my life I shall exchange good questions for better ones.

But we must notice another kind of doubt that is not an expression of faith, but a barrier to faith. And the country of this sort of doubt is not a place we should choose to dwell in. It is a place we should pass through, grateful for what the journey teaches us.

There are some, for example, who tell me that with the best will in the world, they *can't* believe. They are simply not convinced of the truth of faith. They are not persuaded by the case that is made for it. For them to say that they believe would be a pretense that would rob them of their integrity. Such pretense is not pleasing to God who seeks truth in our inner being, and it is not the sort of behaviour we should encourage. Who is pleased by pretended belief? We are not, for it violates our sense of intellectual honesty. God is not, for He reads our hearts and knows what we truly believe. That is why such unbelief is not culpable unbelief, for it is born in, and it is sustained by, our sense of personal integrity. And yet it is not a place where we should wish to remain, for the appeal of faith is strong. What, then, are we to do?

One of the best things we can do is offer to God the honest intention of our heart and the best attention of our mind. Said Yeats, "All God asks is our attention." And if we give it to Him, and bring our questions to the place where answers may be found, it is His promise that the Spirit will lead us into truth. We should not seek Him at all if some part of us did not in some sense believe already. Indeed, Pascal tells us that we could not seek Him if He had not already found us. But if this is true we can pray honestly, "Lord, I believe; help Thou mine unbelief."

Notice yet another sort of doubt which has less to commend it than the kinds we have just discussed. It is the doubt that persists, not through any lack of clarity, but because of our lack of commitment. We see the truth, but do not do the truth we see. It invites us with a claim we acknowledge to be a rightful claim, yet we will not give ourselves to it. The Spirit speaks, and we hear but will not obey. And this unbelief *is* culpable, for to see the truth and not do it is to become false. It is to lose our integrity, our wholeness. It is to be divided and so lose our integration. It is to die a little. The claim of truth on us is surely that we should obey what we clearly see and acknowledge. Leslie Weatherhead once wrote to his son Kingsley, "I wish I knew the answer, or is it that what one needs is not to know more but guts to do, up to the point of knowing?" Many of us have questions about faith, and we long for deeper understanding. But are we doing up to the point of knowing? Years ago a British Prime Minister remarked that we are always wishing for the wisdom of our forefathers when what we need to do is emulate their courage.

Horace Bushnell was a lecturer in Yale who found himself plagued by doubts and uncertainty. One day he asked himself, "What is the use of my trying to get further knowledge so long as I do not cheerfully yield to what I already know?" He then declared his certainty of the eternal difference between right and wrong and pledged himself to live for the right. He affirmed his belief in God's existence, and pledged himself to do God's will as it was made clear to him. His religious perplexities were not allowed to distract him from his ethical certainties, and he became a wise and saintly man. Not long before he died in Hartford, Connecticut, he told a friend, "I know Jesus Christ better than I know any man in Hartford." Kierkegaard expresses the same insight when he tells us that,

"The highest of all is not to understand the highest but to act upon it."

Dr. Robert McCracken tells of a young man who was having great difficulty with his faith. Everything about it was a problem. If it wasn't the Virgin Birth, it was the Resurrection; if it wasn't the Resurrection it was the Miracles; if it wasn't the Miracles it was the Trinity. Christian belief was one large difficulty. Having heard him express his perplexity for a great many months, his minister asked him one day, "Do you ever have trouble with the Ten Commandments?" It was a shrewd question, and it touched a nerve. The young man became angry and indignant. But when he cooled down he broke down and admitted that he was having great difficulty with certain of the Ten Commandments. His intellectual doubts were an evasion of the real issue, which was moral. It wasn't lack of understanding that was his trouble, but weakness of the will. It was much easier to go on asking questions than it was to face up to answers that required a moral discipline that was difficult.

David Roberts, who held the Chair of Philosophy of Religion at Union Theological Seminary, New York, tells of a man who said to him once, "I spent twenty years trying to come to terms with my doubts. Then one day it dawned on me that I had better come to terms with my faith. Now I have passed from the agony of questions I cannot answer to the agony of answers I cannot escape."

You would not be hearing this today if you did not believe with at least part of yourself. You may feel a little hypocritical about being in church, thinking that your presence affirms too much. Yet you cannot stay away because to do so would be to affirm too little. Give the believing part of you your attention. Nourish it, not only by thinking, but by adoring. Find in yourself what you truly believe, not what you pretend to believe, or would like to believe, or are expected to believe. Discover for yourself that measure of belief which is certain, apart from which you would not be yourself, which is just *you*. The fact is you could not get a razor blade between you and what you truly believe. Start there, and build on that conviction with which you are entirely comfortable because it is expression of your integrity and not a contradiction of it, and you will be brought from what William James called our "torn-to-pieceness" to wholeness.

John Ruskin wrote a letter to his father to tell him how he became a Christian. He said, "I resolved that I would believe in Christ and take Him for my Master in whatever I did . . . that to disbelieve was as difficult as to believe; that there are mysteries either way, but the best mystery was that which gave me Christ for a Master. When I had done this I felt a peace within me which I had never known before."

Alexander White, one of Scotland's greatest preachers, noticed that a famous scientist was attending his services. White resolved that he would do all in his power to win him to membership in the church. For several weeks his sermons were of the sort that would appeal to the scientific mind. Imagine the preacher's delight when the scientist declared his intention to join the congregation. Alexander White asked him what had convinced him that this was something he should do. He thought and, I suppose, hoped that the distinguished new member would speak of his sermons and his preaching. He never mentioned them! Instead, he told how an old woman spoke to him on the steps of the church one Sunday, asking him, quite simply, "Are you a Christian?"

He replied, "I am thinking about it."

"Oh," she said, "Do come further in than that! Jesus Christ means the world to me."

"As I looked at her radiant face with its shining eyes, I knew that she had a secret which I didn't have, and I wanted it with all my heart," said the scientist.

There is much mystery either way, but the best mystery is that which gives us Christ for a Saviour, for it is a mystery we can trust and not be disappointed. Don't be satisfied until you have moved from the doubt that is a barrier to faith to the questions that are an expression of it. For such questions leave us lost, not in perplexity, but in wonder, love and praise. It is like leaving the wilderness for the Promised Land!

COME OUT THE WILDERNESS!
PART III

PERMIT ME VOYAGE

St. Matthew 4:1-11

In earlier sermons we noticed that a wilderness experience is one we should pass through. We went on to describe some of the experiences in which we should not dwell, but from which we should emerge: From guilt to forgiveness; from justifying ourselves to expressing ourselves; from doubt to faith.

It would be helpful if we made a list of our own recognized wilderness experiences. Some of them we have passed through already, moving from desert to green pastures. Others are yet to be left behind as we continue our pilgrimage. Remember that it is enormously helpful simply to recognize the wilderness nature of some experiences. And now, let me mention several more.

1. *We must get beyond surviving to living.*

When asked what he did during the French Revolution, Emmanuel Joseph Sieyès is alleged to have answered, "I survived!" And that is a very good thing to do in times of violent revolution. To survive is as much as anyone has a right to ask of us, or that we have a right to expect of ourselves, when times are critical or out of joint. But to survive would be a poor expression of our best hope. Surely we aspire not only to survive, but to go beyond survival to fulfillment. We wish not only to survive, but to be happy, contented, creative. Indeed, that is not only our hope, it is an expression of our values. Albert

98

Camus once said that survival is the ultimate value for animals. I'm not sure he is right about that. Some animal parents will sacrifice their own lives to protect their young, and thus express a care higher than their instinct for survival. But Camus is certainly right when he goes on to say that the human animal transcends the instinct to survive and that we are willing to lose our lives for some higher cause or value, whether truth, love, our country or peace. Sometimes we decide to die *for* something, not merely *of* something.

When Camus said that, he put himself in very good company. Our Lord said it, too, in words of unforgettable power and beauty: "If a man will allow himself to be lost for my sake he will find his true self." There it is, the promise of a higher self when we get beyond surviving to living, even if our living is the discovery of something worth dying for. We enter into life by losing our fear of death.

Now, New Yorkers should know this, because they have been well instructed in the matter. One of our largest financial institutions tells us that we should use the services they offer, and not any other, because "for New Yorkers it is not enough to survive; they want to succeed." Indeed they do, but the desire to do so does not belong only to New Yorkers, it is the human condition. Who would wish merely to survive when they might succeed? We want to succeed; except that sometimes what we describe as success appears to me to be little more than survival. We measure success by the homes we live in, the amount of money we have and the measure of power we can exercise. But surely shelter, food and security are not success but what it takes to survive. Having them, we ask ourselves, "What lack I yet?" As our Lord said in one of the parables that addresses the issue, we can make a more than adequate living and still miss life.

Years ago, Karl Barth complained that most liberal commentaries on the Bible stop just where they should start. They discuss the authorship, date, origin and destination of the book of the Bible that is their interest, and, having reached their often tentative conclusions, think that their work is done. Barth says it is only beginning. They must go on to ask what the author says, what is the book's message, and how God speaks to us through it.

We do something like that with our lives. We work hard to achieve security, an adequate measure of provision and comfort for our dear ones, and think that is all there is to it, that we have achieved the goal, the "end" of life. Our Lord does not agree with us that these things are the goal of life. They make life possible but they are not what it is *for*. He asks us how our life reaches beyond them. *Does* it reach beyond them? T. S. Eliot forces the question on us by asking, "Where is the life that we have lost in living?" and Robertson Davies will tell anyone who will listen to him that we can be successful in making a living and fail life.

Here is a bit of irony worth noticing, one of God's little jokes, what Blake would call "fearful symmetry": It is when we are most concerned about survival that we are least likely to survive!

Our school rugby coach, who knew as much about life as he did about rugby football, used to say that it is the player who is trying hardest not to get hurt who is most likely to get hurt. Stiff and tight from fear of injury, he seems more vulnerable, more susceptible to injury. But the player who participates with a reckless abandon stays loose and bears the shock of colliding bodies with greater ease and safety.

Sport provides us with another illustration that makes our point. The team that comes to a game hoping to survive will almost certainly lose. You don't play to survive, you play to win. If a fighter's highest aim is to survive the contest, he'll lose. To beat your opponent, you have to come to win.

Notice how that principle applies in your job. What is your best hope for it, your goal? Is it retirement? To hang in there long enough to receive a pension? If that's what you're after, of course you'll play it safe; you will be cautious and take no risks. And whether you notice it or not, you'll begin to die long before you're dead. You will lose your edge; you will cease to be interesting; your initiative will leave you; you may even sell your integrity for security. It's not simply that you may lose yourself; it is that you may never discover who you are or what you might have accomplished. Yet those very qualities of energy, initiative, and creativity, sacrificed for survival, are the values that would have gone far to ensure your success.

"Surviving" will dry you up and shrivel you. It may rob you of your self-respect. Imagine coming to the end of your life's work and saying with a sense of relief, "Retirement! I did it! That was my goal and I reached it!" Of course you will reach it. All it takes to reach it is time. But what did you stand for? What standard did you raise? What values did you affirm? What difference did you make? Now that you've done it, was it worth doing? If you had to do it again, wouldn't you think less about survival and more about living?

When I consider my own life, I am haunted by insights that converge from several sources. I think, for example, of the notes Nathaniel Hawthorne wrote in his diary planning a novel (which, incidentally, was never written) "in which the chief character never appears." That comes close to the bone, doesn't it? Some of us feel that our lives are a bit like that. We have survived, but we sometimes wonder if the chief character has ever appeared.

Or I think of the title Caitlin Thomas gave the book she wrote after her husband Dylan's death. She called it *Leftover Life To Kill*. Nothing to do, then, but get the time in. No "end" in the sense of purpose, only the end that finishes everything.

I think, too, of poignant words written by Rabindranath Tagore, "The music I came to sing remains unsung. I have spent my days stringing and unstringing my instrument." How terribly sad — to have music in us, and not sing it! To survive, but without melody! To exist, but with no song!

Survival is one of those things you can have only if you go after something else, something better. It is like justice. The only way to have justice is to love mercy. Justice is possible only when it is transcended. It is like our humanity, which is safe only when it is attached to divinity.

Some years ago a film called "Seven Beauties" received a great deal of serious attention. The title was misleading, because the movie was a study of survival in a Nazi concentration camp. The "hero" survived the brutality of the camp by becoming as demonic as those who ran it. The film ends when the man who has sacrificed every human value to save his own skin says, "Yes, I am alive." But the word "alive" has about it all the coldness and emptiness of death. When he claims life, he talks like a dead man.

Now, Bruno Bettleheim said that the movie's thesis is false, and Victor Frankel agrees with Bettleheim. They, too, were prisoners in concentration camps, but they tell us that those who survived did so, not because surviving was their supreme value, but because they had human, transcendent and even religious values which raised them beyond mere survival and enabled them to retain their dignity and discover meaning in all the degradation they had to endure. This is a testimony to the greatness of the human spirit which in the worst conditions imaginable is not content merely to survive, but seeks to preserve the values which make and keep us human. Isn't it one of the terrible ironies of our time that the meaning of freedom has been best understood, not by those of us who have it, but by the prisoners in the Gulag who had it taken from them and yet could write the meaning of it on scraps of toilet paper smuggled out to instruct and inspire us?

In the awful winter of 1940–1941, Edward R. Murrow sent frequent messages from Britain to America describing the appalling destruction and suffering of the blitz. He ended one of his broadcasts by saying, "Nevertheless there is a glory about it because we have lived a life, not an apology." What could be sadder than making the one life we have add up to little more than an apology?

2.   *We must move from fear to fun, leaving behind our dread of God, and learning to enjoy Him.*

The religious experience of many of you has been one of terror. You were afraid of God. Perhaps some of you still are. It has put its mark on your life, and you have longed to move from that sense of dread to something more gracious and loving.

Yet there are many Christians who think that to fear God is the proper religious attitude. It seems to be scriptural, for the

Bible speaks often of "the fear of the Lord." Job tells us that the fear of the Lord is the beginning of wisdom. Perhaps this sense of dread is not anything to be left behind, but the appropriate feeling for us to have towards God. Perhaps it is not a wilderness experience to pass through, but a place in which we ought to dwell.

The Bible speaks often of "the fear of the Lord," and exhorts us to possess it. But when it does, the meaning is not that we should be afraid of God, terrified of Him as One from whom harm could come to us. What the Bible calls "the fear of the Lord" is close to what we should call reverence. It is not a fear characterized by terror, but an adoration filled with awe and wonder. When Job says that to fear God is the beginning of wisdom he means that to revere, to respect, to give our adoration to Him, is to be wise enough to put first the things that ought to be first. It means that we do not idolize money, or power, or ambition, but ascribe value to the truth and goodness we see in God. To "fear" God in this sense is to love Him supremely and ascribe worth to Him above all else that might claim our worship.

Job rightly perceives and declares that it is the beginning of wisdom to fear God in this way, for it means that we give our reverence to those things that are worthy of it. Otherwise we "spend our money for that which is not bread, and our labor for that which satisfieth not." And that is foolish, not wise. In other words, to give reverence to God, and to adore Him, is to put first in our life what is worthy of first place and ought to have first place. It enables us, at the very least, to have a right sense of values. To give to God our worship is to praise what is worthy of our praise. It is to put our reverence where it properly belongs.

We should also notice those parts of the Bible that tell us quite plainly that we should not be afraid of God because God loves us and desires that we should trust and love and rejoice in Him. Indeed, if we love God how can we fear Him? "Perfect love casts out fear."

Jesus talked a great deal about fear. We talk far more about sin than about fear. Dr. Frederic Greeves in his book *The*

Meaning of Sin tells us that, allowing for parallel accounts, our Lord used the noun on only six occasions and the verb on only three occasions in the first three Gospels. But Bishop Stephen Neil in his fine book, *A Genuinely Human Existence*, tells of a German scholar who with characteristic thoroughness counted the occasions on which the Scriptures exhort us not to be afraid. He found ninety-nine instances. The words echo and re-echo through the Book, "Don't be afraid!"

Why does our Lord, and why do the writers of the Gospels, speak so much about fear and so little about sin? They do so because much of our sin is rooted in our fear. When we cannot have the good opinion of someone we come very near to hating him. And many of us have been afraid of God because we thought we could not have His good opinion of us, and have come very near to hating Him. Out of that fear, resentment, and grievance has come much of our disobedience. Such emotions and attitudes inevitably give rise to hostility and estrangement. That is the meaning of sin. Sin is that which separates us from God. Much of it has its roots in the fear which make it impossible for us to love and trust Him.

When our Lord tells us not to be afraid, then, it is no casual word of easy reassurance; it's not just a bit of positive thinking. It strikes at the very root of our fallen condition. It is the expression of all that He came to overcome. For the work of Jesus is God's way of convincing us that we don't need to be afraid of Him. How can we be afraid in the face of so perfect a love? The words and works of Jesus, His life and His death, are God's way of so showing us Himself that we are moved from suspicion, resentment, and hostility to love, trust and joy.

Indeed, the lives of the saints tell us they travelled not only through fear to faith, but beyond reverence to joy, to what I have called "fun." I call it "fun" because often we Christians make Christian joy such a solemn thing that there is no fun in it.

There is a great sentence by Coventry Patmore which he puts into the mouth of a little midge:

Shall I, a gnat which dances in Thy ray,
    Dare to be reverent?

Patmore has already told us that love raises the spirit above
the sphere even of reverence, to laughter. He knows, and has
the gnat tell us, that one of the highest expressions of faith is
the love that is so sure of God that it wants to dance in His
presence. Some of the most "reverent" people I know are unbelievers who have retained enough superstition and suspicion
to make them solemnly reverent when all vital belief has van-
ished. Someone once said of one, that he was "reverent enough
to be an unbeliever."

Dante described the music of heaven as the "laughter of
the universe." Did you know that the Eastern Church calls
Easter "God's laughter"? Does that strike a false note for you?
Does it seem alien to your faith? It ought not to, for the *words*
are familiar to us; it is just that we haven't believed them
enough to take them seriously. Instead of taking them seriously we take them solemnly, and spoil them. We sing, "Him
serve with mirth, His praise forth tell," but the way we do it
hasn't much mirth in it, and while the *words* are there, the
lightsomeness is missing. Have we forgotten that one of the
greatest statements of our reformed tradition is that our chief
end is "to glorify God and to *enjoy* Him forever?"

Let me ask you: have you ever, even once in your life,
praised God with mirth? Do you have any sense of fun in your
faith? Do you *enjoy* God? We think that if we did, we should be
failing to take our faith seriously enough. But surely the best
way to take it seriously is to believe what it says. And what it
says is that we please God, not when we're afraid of Him, but
when we delight in Him.

What we really mean when we say we don't take our faith
seriously enough is that we don't take it solemnly enough. Our
mistake is to think that in order to be serious we must be solemn. But how can we take solemnly the best news in the world,
that we are perfectly loved, eternally sought, graciously forgiven, uniquely cherished? No wonder our Lord likened the
Kingdom of God to a wedding reception! We are taking our
faith seriously when we believe the good will God has for us,
and celebrate it with joy. George MacDonald was entirely
right when he said that "it is the heart that is not yet sure of its

God that is afraid to laugh in His presence." Says C. S. Lewis, "Joy is the serious business of heaven." But it is not solemn. That is why Chesterton tells us that angels fly because they take themselves so lightly!

A good test of the gladness of our faith is to ask ourselves what we feel when the thought of God comes unexpectedly to our mind. To suddenly think of God should be like catching sight of our own dear children when we didn't expect to see them. Our face lights up with the delight of seeing one who is so precious to us. How can we love and not delight in the one we love? Charles Wesley got it right. He wrote, "My heart it doth dance at the sound of His name"!

To move from fear to fun is not only to enjoy God's delight in us, but to catch His playfulness in creation. Chesterton tells us that we are mistaken to speak of the "work" of creation. Creation is not work, it is play. He tries to recapture for us our lost sense of God's playfulness by telling us that the sun does not rise by Natural Law, but because every morning God likes to say to it, "Get up and do it again!" "Do you know why there are so many daisies?" asks Chesterton. He goes on to say that, like a little child making daisy-chains, God makes so many daisies because He loves to multiply beautiful things. God declares to Job that at the creation of the world "the morning stars sang together and all the sons of God shouted for joy." It may be, says Chesterton, that God is the only child left in the universe.

3. *Finally, we must move through Time to the Eternal.*

Do you remember the opening sentence of *Pilgrim's Progress*? Bunyan wrote, "As I walked through the wilderness of this world." That's it! We say that this world is a wilderness, not to diminish its splendor, but to be reconciled to its transience. We are but strangers and pilgrims upon the earth, finding here no abiding city but seeking one that is to come. I mean the heavenly one.

There is a saying of Jesus which some scholars believe to be genuine, but which is not recorded in the New Testament. Inscribed on the wall of a mosque near Delhi, it reads, "Jesus, on whom be peace, has said: 'This world is a bridge. Pass over it. But do not build your dwelling there.' "

That saying is consistent with our Lord's teaching. He told a parable once about a man who gave his steward his notice. Soon the man would be out of a job. What did the steward do? He began at once to plan for the time when he would no longer be employed. He started to use his connections to ensure his future. He started putting people under obligation to him by doing them favors. They would "owe him one," as we would say, and he would collect later. Sounds logical! The master commended the man for his shrewdness and resourcefulness. But the point of the parable is that we are not as wise as the steward. We go on behaving as though we are going to dwell in this world forever and make no attempt to prepare ourselves for the time when our earthly pilgrimage will be over. We build on the bridge instead of passing over it. We regard this matcrial world as our permanent dwelling-place. But if we do, and if all our values are material values, then in the end we shall lose them all.

I flew to Italy once and discovered that Canadian currency isn't any good there. I know one of the wealthiest men in Canada. He is not only very wealthy, he is very old and won't be around much longer. Do you know how he is spending his time and energy? Fighting with his children. About money! And power! And real estate! And shares! You would think he is going to live forever! He has no sense at all of his pilgrim status. Yet who would want to live on a bridge? To build on a bridge is to suffer from the worst sort of confusion.

When I read Bunyan's words about passing through the wilderness of this world, they do two things for me. They make this world more precious because I am passing through it. Every Spring is more welcome, and every Fall more cherished. Dear familiar faces are more beautiful and all human love and kindness and joy more wonderful. Every opportunity to love and trust and cherish is to be welcomed and seized, for it is one of a limited number.

More important, it gives me all sorts of hints, promises and intimations of that other Land. It reminds me that every night we pitch our moving tent a day's march nearer Home. Such experiences help me know what heaven will be like. Walking through the wilderness of this world, I always sense I'm a stranger here. I love this world tenderly and should think it ungrateful if I were not to celebrate its splendor. But I have needs it cannot meet and longings it cannot satisfy. Plato tells us that this world is but a faint shadow of the eternal, spiritual world. But it is more than a shadow, it is a promise. It tells me that I belong to another world which is my true home, and that one day I shall dwell there. And it gives me strong hints of what it is like.

A woman and the missionary she was visiting in a lonely outpost in India watched the sun go down. "What a splendid sunset!" the missionary exclaimed. And the woman replied, "Yes, and in such a tiny place!" But what does it matter how tiny the place is if it reveals to us the glory of the evening? And what does it matter how transient this dear world of ours is if in its weaker glories we can spy "some shadow of eternity." C. S. Lewis remarks somewhere that if the most beautiful musical phrase imaginable could be made into a word, then the word would be an adjective, not a noun. It would describe something more splendid still; it would be one beauty pointing beyond itself to the ultimate Beauty. All my life has been the finding of magnificent adjectives describing a Glory I have not yet seen.

Christians know this, for we believe that the Eternal has come to meet us. This tiny world is the place of God's redeeming action. What we have longed for offers itself to us now and forever. Says Malcolm Muggeridge, "In the human heart Time and Eternity meet." And to have Him, to have our Lord Christ, is to dwell in the Eternal now. It is to Him that we go. Christ is the life of heaven, as Christ is our life here and now. It is in His love that we dwell, and it is to His love that we journey.

That is why I have made the lovely words of Hart Crane and James Agee my prayer of pilgrimage. They not only remind us that we are pilgrims, but declare the nature of our destination:

"Permit me voyage, Love, into your Hands,"

We move from Love to Love.
    God grant you journeying mercies!

HOW TO BE INDIGNANT

Our sense of indignation is both inevitable and useful. It is inevitable because we have a moral sense and because it is the work of faith to sharpen its perceptions and deepen its sensitivity. Our moral sense commends what is right and good so that when its values are violated we become indignant.

It is not only inevitable, it is useful. A sense of indignation has provided much of the energy that has reformed our society, and has produced some of our greatest literature and music. We see this very clearly in Jonathan Swift. If you ever visit his grave in St. Patrick's Cathedral, Dublin, you will notice his unusual epitaph. He composed it himself: "Here he lies where his furious indignation can no longer lacerate his heart." Very powerful words, and true of the man who was lacerated by a furious indignation all his life and turned it to very good and wholesome account by what he did and by what he wrote. Who, having read it, can ever forget his "Modest Proposal" for dealing with the Irish poor?

If our sense of indignation is inevitable and useful, then surely it would be a serious thing to lose it, or the awareness that makes it. What sort of person would you be if nothing could make you angry, if you no longer cared and so lost the power to be morally indignant? What would it say of your conscience and your compassion? Living in New York City, it would be easy to allow the violence, abrasiveness and rudeness we encounter day by day to coarsen us so that we became used to it, took it for granted, regarded it as normal and accepted it without protest.

That does happen to us. We grow accustomed to violence and homelessness as we get used to the noise and pace of this great city. And then some incident occurs — a young policeman is shot, or a young mother murdered, and our sense of

110

outrage blazes for a while until it dies down again. Much in New York is beautiful, wholesome and excellent. But the good things in New York constitute no problem for us. The problem is that we can easily become coarsened by what is vulgar, ugly and wicked. We should be seriously diminished if we were to lose our power of moral indignation and cease to deplore, and come to accept, what is evil.

We see this deep sense of moral outrage in the life of our Lord. How could He care so deeply about people and *not* be angry at how they were treated? Time and again His indignation was kindled against those who laid heavy burdens on others which they themselves would not bear. Then, of course, He became so furious at the desecration of the Temple in Jerusalem by the dealers and moneychangers that He drove them out with a whip. His Father's name was being dishonored for gain in His own house, and what was the Son to do but drive out those who dishonored it? So His indignation blazed forth and He emptied the place. That bothers some Christians who think that anger is always wrong. It seems to me to be perfectly appropriate, knowing the things He felt deeply about. His action affords us a splendid example of righteous indignation. We should be depleted personalities and lacking in character if nothing ever made us angry.

Yet as soon as this is said, we must qualify it. You see, our moral indignation shares the ambiguity of all things human. It is neither as pure, righteous or single-minded as we like to suppose. We have to keep a careful eye on it. Don't we *like* to be indignant? There is something in our sense of moral outrage that does not displease us. What a sense of superiority, of virtue, it gives us! It flatters our conceit to occupy the moral high ground. It is then we need to remember that when we take the moral high ground we have further to fall, that our indignation is not always righteous indignation, and that even though we may be in the right, we are seldom as right as we think we are. Knowing ourselves, we know that our indignation travels all the way from bad temper, petulance, and irritability to the reforming zeal of Wilberforce, or Shaftesbury, or Lincoln, or Martin Luther King. Always it is wise to examine the *quality* of our indignation. We should examine it not in the moment of indignation, usually, for then we are too busy being indignant to analyze it thoughtfully. But later, in a quieter moment, we may usefully assess our feelings and our actions.

Preachers, as you know, are prone to moral indignation. Reinhold Niebuhr used to say that his degree of it was in direct relation to the size of his congregation. The larger the crowd, the more indignant he became about the world's evils. What do preachers tell themselves when they try to determine the quality of their indignation? Let me invite you to overhear what one preacher says to himself.

I. *Let your indignation be softened by humility.*

It's easy to be indignant with other people and forget that we ourselves are part of the evil that arouses our sense of outrage. King David was like that. He became very angry when Nathan the prophet told him about a rich man who, having many sheep of his own, stole a poor man's only lamb. David was so angry at the covetousness of it, and at the rich man's lack of pity, that he declared that the man should be put to death for his wickedness. It was then that Nathan said, "Thou art the man!" All the time he had been describing David's own sin, and the King hadn't even recognized it. *Now* he sees it, for Nathan has made it clear. The prophet speaks the same words to us: "Thou art the man!" Too often in our indignation we forget that we are implicated in the very evils we deplore. Who can forget the way in which Thackeray revealed how the judge is guilty of the offence for which he passes sentence on the prisoner; the teacher is guilty of the laziness for which she punishes her pupil; and the preacher is guilty of the sins for which he condemns his congregation.

Some time ago I preached a sermon called "Only Not Through Me!" It was preached from some powerful words of Solzhenitsyn who, seeing how we are deceived by The Lie, declares, "Let The Lie come into the world. Let it even reign supreme. Only not through me!" That is a useful and necessary thing to say in these days when we have lost our awareness of our own dimensions, and a sense of what we stand for. But we must remember that we are part of the lie we resolve to resist. We, too, are imperfect at levels both clear to us and hidden from us. We are not only the solution, we are the problem, and it is wise to be aware of it. If we are not, we become self-righteous and are guilty of pretension and conceit.

I remember this when I express my disappointment with the church. Do you know what disappoints me after forty years in the ministry? That offered so much grace, there is so little graciousness; so much truth to welcome, and we remain false; so much light to illumine, and our lives are still dark; so much to elevate and enlarge us, and we are still petty; so much mercy, and still we are merciless. I look over the congregation and see this. How easy to be indignant about it!

Except that I see the same failure every morning when I look in the mirror. There are dark places in my life where the light does not shine, and I, too, am often graceless, petty and unkind. To remember it softens my indignation, or at least gathers me into it with others.

Years ago, a British daily newspaper offered a prize for the best letter answering the question, "What is wrong with the world?" The winning letter was also the shortest. It said, "Dear Sir, I am!" and it was signed, "G. K. Chesterton." Let your indignation be softened by humility.

II.   *Let your indignation be matched by your responsibility.*

F. W. Robertson used to warn that it is a dangerous enterprise to kindle an emotion that is not expressed in action. It is dangerous to the health of the soul to have truth and not be obedient to it. That man is already half false who allows his emotions to carry him where his will and actions will not follow. To have the truth and not honor it is worse than ignorance, for we cannot plead ignorance as our excuse. We are false who feel deeply about important things and do nothing.

Robertson then goes on to say that this is particularly true of our religious life and of religious people. Our feelings are often kindled by our worship, by the singing of moving hymns, and by the power of the Scriptures and the eloquence of the preacher. This is good and healthy so long as our deep feelings find some expression in responsible action. But that doesn't always happen. The words are spoken, the hymns sung, the lessons read, and we are moved. But not to deeds that express the truth we have seen. Our emotions rise, and then they fall, and nothing much has changed.

Haven't you noticed, for example, that we would rather feel angry at things than change the things that anger us? We would rather blame God for the ills that afflict us than minister to the afflicted. Here is a man who comes to me hurt and angry that someone dear to him has died of lung cancer. He demands to know why God allows such things to happen. But surely he is aware that many of our diseases are not in any immediate sense to be blamed on God, but to be labeled "diseases of choice" and blamed on our own foolishness. I read the other day that lung cancer would be reduced by eighty-seven percent if people didn't smoke. Some of our sexually-transmitted diseases have to do with the lifestyle we choose, are closely related to our sexual morality or lack of it. Heart disease is affected by our diet. We smoke too much, eat too much, drink too much, take too little exercise, and complain to God when our dear ones are victims of diseases largely within their control. This is not true of all forms of cancer or heart disease, but it is true of some of them. We know this. But it is easier to be indignant than to be disciplined. We'd rather find someone to blame for what happens to us than accept responsibility for ourselves.

The same is true of some of the social ills that afflict our society. We look at the homeless, or the poor, or those who suffer from famine or pestilence, and wonder why God allows it. Yet we know that in our own wallet, or bank account, we have the means to alleviate these injustices a little. Complaint is cheap; to accept responsibility is costly. So we choose to complain. But our indignation is hollow and hypocritical if we do not attempt to redeem the evils we complain about.

Sometimes I think about the cities of California and the shifting earth on which they are built. We have known the risk of it for years. Yet if the earth does shift, bringing death and destruction, what a questioning of the wisdom and goodness of God there will be! How many will immediately make the problem a religious one, asking why God allows such things to happen, and blaming Him for them. Surely such indignation is better directed against our own ordering of things rather than the divine ordering of things. He has, after all, made us responsible beings.

It seems to me there are two sorts of answers to the problem of suffering and evil. One is a theodicy, a reasoned defence which seeks to justify the ways of God to men. That answer can be helpful and useful, and it has been attempted in every age by the best minds of faith. But there is an answer of another sort. It does not so much seek to justify God's ways as to make us the instruments of them. I should think that Mother Teresa does not spend much time asking why little children die, and she spends no time at all blaming God for it. Rather, seeing them die one by one, she saves them one by one. She doesn't ask for an answer, she becomes the answer, or part of it. Her compassion matches her indignation. Her anger becomes the servant of her love. We cannot remind ourselves too often that while we cannot do everything it is better to do something than to do nothing.

III.   *Let your indignation be instructed by realism.*

I must tell myself this frequently, for I am a romantic, a dreamer, and grasped by the optimism of grace. I often need a good dose of realism to sober me.

I thought of our need for realism the other day as I walked down Madison Avenue and saw in a shop window a printed card which said, "We support the movement for democracy in China." That is a calm statement. I wonder out of what fury and indignation it came forth. I can imagine the anger that produced it, for we all felt it. The slaughter by the Chinese communists of their own brightest young people in Beijing has been an outrage to the conscience of us all. For the last several weeks, at the close of worship, those who were born in China, or have dear ones there, or love its people and its history and culture, have come to me, sick at heart, to pour out their grief and indignation. What are we to do about it? We feel helpless, and all we can do is speak of it, and speak out against it, and make the leaders of our nation aware of the indignation we feel and which they share. And we march and demonstrate. We *must* do these things to give some expression to the anger we feel.

But when we have done so we must not feel that we have done much. We are tempted to think that our words and demonstrations accomplish more than they do. We must remind ourselves that our outrage has changed nothing in China, for a regime that is capable of gunning down its own young people is not likely to be deeply moved, or in any way changed, by protesters of a different ideology on the other side of the world. The cruelty of the communists had already been seen in Tibet where they sought to wipe out the Tibetan people. We should have learned something from that, and allowed it to shape our hopes and expectations.

Some years ago Shirley McLaine visited China and returned to this country speaking of how deeply moved she had been by what she called the "benevolent totalitarianism" she found there. A "benevolent totalitarianism"? Now, that's a good phrase, except that the words are a contradiction. Have we not yet learned that totalitarian governments are not interested in benevolence, only in power — the getting of it and keeping of it. We are naive if we do not recognize that, and allow the recognition of it to inform our attitudes and shape our actions. Lady Astor was more astute than Shirley McLaine when, having been introduced to Josef Stalin she asked, "When are you going to stop killing people?" He killed over thirty million of his own people! That is more than the present population of Canada.

We welcome every sign of better relations with the Soviet Union. Of course we are gladdened by every gesture of good will, by every initiative for peace, by every meeting of leaders that seeks to make our world safe. But we must not be naive. Indignation is not enough. Words are not enough. Preachers sometimes think that when they have preached about a troublesome issue they have resolved it. What a relief to get it off one's chest! How searching our insight and wise our conclusion! But we easily deceive ourselves. Evil is more intractable than we like to think. One sermon, or protest, or demonstration, accomplishes little. If we are in it at all, we'd better be in it for the long haul. Our indignation may be inevitable and useful, but it will be more valuable if we do not overestimate its power. Always we should follow our easy indignation with a hard question, "What more needs to be *done*?"

IV.   *Measure your indignation by its breadth as well as by its intensity.*

Of course our indignation must be focussed, for we can't be indignant about everything all the time. Yet sometimes our moral outrage is too narrow.

Most obviously, it is too narrow when we are indignant only about those wrongs that touch us. We are perfectly capable of putting up with injustice so long as we are not the victims of it. I have often noticed that for some of us the problem of suffering is no problem at all until it touches flesh of our flesh and bone of our bone. Suddenly we demand, "Why should this happen to me?" Yet suffering is a problem not just when it happens to us, but when it happens to anyone. If it happens to anyone, why shouldn't it happen to you or me?

There are some words which will not allow us to limit them. Justice is one. Once the word is free it cannot be restricted to one group or class or nation. Injustices are not evil only when I am afflicted by them, but when anyone is afflicted by them. That is one reason why our indignation must have some breadth to it.

Martin Niemoller, describing his experience in Germany before the Second World War, tells us that the Nazis came for the Communists, but he did not speak out, for he was not a Communist. Then they came for the Jews, and he had nothing to say because he was not a Jew. They came, then, for the Trade Unionists, but why would he say anything when he wasn't a Trade Unionist? They came next for the Catholics, but he was a Protestant. Then they came for him, and by that time there was nobody left to say anything.

We too narrowly focus our indignation in another way. We become people of one cause. Now that can be a useful narrowing of concern. But sometimes it makes us uncharitable to others who have their own particular concerns and do not share ours. Their indignation is not aroused by the same issues that kindle ours. We think that our cause should be everybody's cause, and when others do not share our concern or match its intensity, we dismiss them as lacking in moral seriousness. If others do not seek our goals, our indignation must be wise enough to know that other people may be seeking different ends, or the same ends by different means. We must leave room for them. Surely there are enough good causes to go round! Too many good people have become the victims of the inordinate zeal of the person of one cause.

Sometimes this selectivity of our moral indignation becomes hypocritical. Not long ago, the Province of Canada in which I lived for thirty years banned the importation of wines from South Africa. I presume the intention was to make a statement about apartheid. That may have been a useful thing for the government to do, for apartheid is a very wicked thing indeed. But the gesture cost the government nothing. It made no difference at all to its revenues. Yet at the time it imposed a ban on South African wines, it continued to allow Russian cars to be brought into the country and sold there. And Russia, all the while, was carrying out a policy of genocide in Afghanistan. Now, I couldn't put that together, can you? We used to say, "What's sauce for the goose is sauce for the gander." But not in this matter, apparently. Sometimes the selectivity of our moral indignation reveals our own prejudices, and our own interests. Sometimes it is the expression, not of moral principle, but of political expediency.

V.   *Remember that your moral indignation draws its integrity from its costliness.*

Count the cost! If your outrage costs you nothing, be suspicious of it. If it is going to cost you something, know what it is, measure it carefully, and be prepared to pay it. Jesus did. When He threw out of the Temple those who dishonored it, He knew that it meant His life. As soon as He did it, His enemies quickened their intention to do away with Him. That was the cost of what He did, and He knew it, and He paid it. But I am sometimes ashamed of the indignation that costs nothing. It is too cheap to be authentic.

A few years ago, the Government of British Columbia fired a number of civil servants in an attempt to reduce the cost of government. I don't know whether or not they were justified in doing so, but, justified or not, those who lose their jobs began at once to demonstrate in front of the government buildings. They had a perfect right to do so, for ours is a free society. On banners made to carry in their protest, some had the word, "Solidarity."

Now that is a noble word. Those who first called themselves by it paid dearly for it. They were imprisoned, tortured, and some were killed. The word came to represent the costliness of freedom, justice and the dignity of the human spirit. Not so in British Columbia. There it cost nothing, and a great word was cheapened by those who used it. There is no place on earth where it is safer to demonstrate against the actions of a government than it is in British Columbia. The integrity of Solidarity in Poland was derived from its costliness. It was an act of enormous insensitivity to take that costly word and cheapen it. The workers in British Columbia were not worthy of the company they claimed to be in.

I grow weary of preachers who speak of "risk." If I had my way, I would forbid any minister to use the word for the next five years. I know ministers who take risks with other people's faith, and I know ministers who take risks with the well-being of the church. But I know very few who take any risk that might mean personal loss. We must all join the Pension Plan. In the past year I have learned more about risk from the young people in New York than I learned in the Christian Ministry in thirty years. These young people come to this intimidating city because more than anything else in the world they want to sing, act, paint or dance; and to do so they drive cabs or become waiters, janitors or parking lot attendants, working at all hours of the day and night in order to do what they most want to do. Their sincerity is proved by its costliness. I admire them enormously. But some ministers have the conceit to think they are courageous in what they say knowing all the time that they speak from a consensus which is the source of their opinions and their courage. How rare is the truly non-conforming man! If you want to encounter one, read about Malcolm Muggeridge and learn what he said and what it cost him. Let us be suspicious of an indignation that costs nothing, whether we meet it in ourselves or encounter it in others.

VI. *Let your indignation be the servant of your purpose.*

Sometimes our sense of outrage simply carries us away. We act first and think later, and sometimes our anger stands up well under our scrutiny. Whatever the consequences, we could not forbear. There was a trembling in our bones and we could not remain silent. We had to speak. We must be careful not to so control our indignation that it loses all its fierceness and spontaneity.

But sometimes I have indulged my indignation, and it has not served me well. I was angry with someone and lost all influence with them. Patience or restraint would have served me better. It was *very* satisfying to allow my irritation to show and to speak the indignant words. But the satisfaction quickly passed, and the regret endured.

The definition of power which seems to me to be the only one worth having, is that power is the ability to achieve purpose. Now, anger always *looks* powerful. When we are angry we are unified and dominant. Yet often what looks like strength because it is loud and aggressive proves to be weakness because it doesn't do what we want it to do. Indeed, it may work against what we wish to accomplish. Power is the ability to achieve purpose, and however impressive it may seem, our anger is weakness if it does not do what we want it to do.

So consider well what it is you want to accomplish; and

before you indulge yourself by giving expression to the indignation you feel, remember that to do so is childish, puerile, if it hinders your purpose. Turn your anger to some good end. Said Martin Luther, "When I am angry, I pray and preach well." Make your indignation your servant, for it can be a foolish master.

We really do have a splendid example in all this. For God is not merely indignant with sin, He redeems it. And He does so by what looks like weakness and foolishness. What could be more helpless than a baby in a manger and a crucified carpenter? Yet by this means God accomplishes His purpose and reconciles us to Himself. For those with eyes to see, this is the power of God and the wisdom of God. For His indignation is His saving grace.

THE TEMPTATION TO BE CHRISTIAN

Christians believe but are sometimes tempted to unbelief. A splendid text in the New Testament says it so plainly: "Lord I believe, help Thou mine unbelief." We believe and are tempted to unbelief and wish it were not so. We'd like to believe with singleness of mind and wholeness of heart. Sometimes we think it would be a relief if we were unbelievers, because then the temptation to unbelief would be removed. We forget that unbelievers are not unbelievers with their whole heart. Unbelievers, too, are tempted. They are tempted to believe. They are tempted to be Christian.

Not long ago somebody said to me of a mutual acquaintance, "He is trying very hard *not* to be a Christian." I know a man who late in life became a Christian to the astonishment of many. But I knew what he had written over the last fifty years and knew that his was no sudden conversion. His whole life has been the story of his temptation to be Christian, until at last he yielded and gave his life to Christ.

There are several instances of this in the New Testament. Here is a lawyer, for example, serious and perceptive, who listens to our Lord answering questions. Noticing how well He answers, he commends our Lord's words. Jesus says to him, "You are not far from the Kingdom."

Here is another bright young man who comes to Him and asks, "Master, what must I do to have eternal life?" And our Lord tells him to go and sell what he has and give it to the poor. He then calls him to discipleship: "Come! Follow me!" He says. The young man went away sadly, but in that moment he was sorely tempted to be a Christian.

And then there is Nicodemus, the older man, the wise one, who came to Jesus by night, secretly, in the soft, mystical night air, to inquire of the young Galilean preacher how one may enter the Kingdom of God. We don't really know all that took place at their meeting, but we do know that much later Nicodemus helped to anoint the body of our Lord for burial, and that on that night when he secretly visited our Lord, Nicodemus was tempted to become a Christian. Do *you* feel the tug of faith, the attraction of it? Do you know the temptation to be Christian?

Some of you would feel uncomfortable, perhaps even a little hypocritical, if you were to affirm the faith. It would seem that you are affirming too much. And yet you would not say that you are an unbeliever. If you were an unbeliever it is unlikely that you would be reading this. You would not call yourself a Christian, and yet you feel the tug of Christian faith. What is it that hunts you and haunts you and attracts you to our Christian way? Let me try to tell you. Of course in so doing I shall simply be describing not only what tempts you to be Christian but what makes and keeps the rest of us Christian.

I. *Notice that one of the things that would tempt me to be a Christian is* **the poverty of the alternatives**.

What else is there to be? Have you thought of that? If not a Christian, then what?

David Roberts tells of a young man who was having a party with a group of his atheistic and agnostic friends. They talked about faith, but only to ridicule it. They talked about belief, but only to diminish it. Yet as this young man listened to their conversation what they said rang a bell for him. But it was not a bell for atheism. It rang a bell for faith. Suddenly, in a moment, he saw the emptiness and futility, the leanness and poverty of the unbelief he shared with them, and in that single moment, when all conversation was directed against faith, he became a Christian.

Do you remember how Chesterton put it in his own whimsical way? He said he never read a word of those who sought to defend Christianity; rather he read the words of the agnostics and the atheists, Spencer and Ingersoll and the rest, and that the more he read the more convinced he became of the truth of

Christianity. He wanted to say to them, "Almost thou persuadest me to be a Christian!"

John Baillie, a distinguished theologian, tells of some of his well-educated friends who have grown uneasy in their unbelief. Once they were assured and certain of it. Now they are less sure because they have become disappointed and disillusioned. Baillie tells us that fifty years ago it was a lot easier to be an unbeliever than it is now. Looking for something to believe in, we could have believed in a kind of mechanistic materialism. It seemed to have some validity. But not any longer. We know now that it is not subtle enough or refined enough to account for human thought and human imagination. It fails before the highest achievements of the human spirit.

It used to be that we might have believed in some kind of evolutionary progress which gave our existence a sense of destiny and optimism. But not any longer. Who would wish to say now with Emile Coué that "every day in every way we are getting better and better?" I should not wish to do so. I have more sympathy with Ogden Nash who tells us that progress was once a very good idea, but it has been going on too long.

Or think of the "isms" of our time, so many related to a humanism that ignores or denies the reality of the spiritual and transcendent. They have no longer any validity for they took too lightly the depth of our depravity and our capacity for evil. We have lost any hope we might once have had in their promises. They were wrong in their analysis, mistaken in their predictions and false in their values. Some years ago the Abbey Theatre in Dublin produced a play with the descriptive title, "The Morning After Optimism." We live in it, this morning after optimism, for many of our hopes have been shattered, and our optimism has given place to despair.

H. G. Wells once wrote a story in which a man must stay alone in a house which he believes to be haunted. The only light he has comes from a number of candles of different lengths. One by one the candles go out until there is only darkness. That is the kind of age in which we are living. We have seen the lights go out one by one, here and there, until one man who rediscovered Jesus says, "If there is no light in Christ then we have no light." Why am I tempted to be a Christian and what makes me one and keeps me one? Simply the poverty of the alternatives. I wouldn't know what else to be. That is one thing. What else?

II. *Surely one of the things that must tempt us to be Christian is the compelling truth of faith.*

Malcolm Muggeridge tells us that there is a very amusing book to be written about how unbelievers explain away the fact that people are still converted to Christianity. When late in his own life he became a Christian, all sorts of explanations were offered of why he had given in. Some said that he had gone soft in the head. Some said he was an old clown who needed a new act. Some said that having enjoyed his sins as a young man, he could abhor them now that he was no longer capable of committing them. So it went on. Every imaginable reason, however far-fetched, was suggested except the correct one. And the correct one was that he became convinced of the truth of faith. It is the *truth* of faith that has been making Christians for two thousand years. Muggeridge came to believe that in the words and Person of Jesus Christ we have the truth of God, the truth of ourselves, the truth of our world. And so he became a Christian.

In this he was a bit like C. S. Lewis. Deeply interested in mythology, in the great Nordic, Germanic, Celtic myths of giants, and gods dying and rising again, at last he became convinced that in Christianity he had found the myth that had come true. It had actually happened. There was a date for it and a place. In other words, what made the two men Christian was the inexpressible, inexhaustible enchantment of Christ. Do you know what makes me and keeps me a Christian? Do you know what tempts you to be one? It is all that you see in Him that is deep and true and beautiful. If He is not our Way, then to whom shall we go to find the way?

Now and then a Professor of English will announce the radical theory that Shakespeare never lived. There was no such person. Now that is enough to startle us and seize our attention. The trouble is, of course, that we still have the plays, and must somehow account for them. So we ask, "Well, if Shakespeare never lived, who wrote the plays?" We are told that it was someone who thought like Shakespeare, who had Shakespeare's insight, his splendid imagination, his power with words. We are told then that Shakespeare never lived but somebody exactly like him did!

Now and then we are told by some radical historian or philosopher that Jesus never lived. But of course we must somehow account for His teaching, the New Testament, the Church and the experience of Christians all through the ages to this very moment. How are we to explain them? If He never lived, where did it all come from? Well, from somebody just like Him! Only one exactly like Him could have done it. If He had not lived, who could have invented Him? And that is His attraction for us. He is inexhaustible. He is unavoidable. Turn from Him? But if we do, to whom shall we go?

When I was little more than a boy, one quiet evening in a church in Belfast, Northern Ireland, I gave my life to Him. It would be easy to make light of that moment of commitment. What did I know of faith or life? But I knew that I loved Him and that I wanted to follow Him. And however little I knew then, there is a direct line between that quiet evening so many years ago and this very moment in which I speak to you. And let me tell you that He means more to me now than He has ever meant at any time in my life. What is it that would tempt me to be Christian? What makes me a Christian and keeps me one? It is the truth of faith. It is the inexhaustible enchantment of Christ.

III.   *Further, the Christ-likeness of other people tempts me to be Christian.*

Not long ago I read of a university professor who as a boy heard Lincoln speak. Lincoln had been his great hero, yet he was terribly disappointed when he began to talk. The President would miss a word here and he would hesitate a bit there.

And then, suddenly, he hit his stride and it all seemed to come together and gather itself with enormous power. This man stood and spoke and his speech became more than mere words. It became "a message in the shape of a man." The boy never forgot it. That's it! The truth of the Gospel becomes a message in the shape of a man, or woman, and then it is doubly compelling. The message and the person come together and you can't deny them, they are so much of a piece.

Saul of Tarsus looked at the face of Stephen, the first Christian martyr, and it shone with the glory of God. Saul never forgot it. Years later King Agrippa looked at Paul, saw the same glory in his face and said, "Almost thou persuadest me to be a Christian!" It is not that Paul *had* a message, he *was* the message. A soldier looked at Florence Nightingale walking in a hospital ward and said to her, "You look like the grace of God!" So it goes on. People gather the truth of Christ into themselves and it becomes so much a part of them that you can't evade their attractiveness, their winsomeness. Dr. Fosdick said once that the life of Jesus was lived like music to be played over again.

Every minister knows A. S. Peake. He was a layman, a splendid teacher who edited a famous commentary on the Bible. One day, years after his teaching had finished, he had a letter from a young man who wrote to thank him for saving his faith. He said that when he was going through a very difficult time, A. S. Peake stood like a barrier between him and unbelief. He ended the letter, "If I may say so, sir, I held on to you while you held on to God."

Who is it that is tempting you to be a Christian? Is it Mother Teresa? Is it your own mother? Is it your wife or husband or your own little girl? By the very goodness of their lives they have become the message. What argument do you have against their saintliness? You look at them and see Jesus! You can't get around them:

> To me 'twas not the truth you taught,
> To you so clear, to me so dim.
> It was that when you came you brought
> A sense of Him.

And from your eyes He beckons me,
And from your heart His love is shed
Till I lose sight of you and see
The Christ instead.

IV. *It is our own experience of the Transcendent.*

Doesn't that tempt you to be a Christian? A famous German theologian was walking on the moors on a misty, grey day, when he came upon a little boy flying a kite. The kite was so high that he couldn't see it. It was out of sight in the mist, in the low cloud. The professor said to the little boy, "How do you know it is there?" And the wee fellow replied at once, "I can feel the pull of it." Not long afterwards, someone asked the professor, "Why do you believe in God and in spiritual Reality?" and he answered in the words of the little fellow with the kite, "I believe because I feel the pull of it."

Haven't you felt the pull of it or sensed the depth of it? Don't you know that there are mysterious altitudes in us? C. Day Lewis, the late Poet Laureate, tells us that no true artist can be a materialist because all truly creative artists know that the sources of their art are too deep for materialism to explain. You know that in you there is music, poetry and a sense of beauty. Living in a city as noisy and as busy as this one, your heart is sometimes melted by the beauty of a poem, the discerning of some radiant truth, the remembrance of a haunting loveliness, or the goodness of a saintly person. The trouble is that we never stop to ask ourselves what kind of people we are that we can be haunted by dreams too beautiful to be untrue and truth too deep for tears. Why is it that, creatures of the earth, we find that earthly things cannot satisfy us? Why is it that we long for the eternal?

C. S. Lewis had experiences transcendent in their joy and beauty, and he pursued them. He said that the whole purpose of his life was to find out where all the beauty came from. His search led him to God. He discovered that all the beauty he had ever experienced was not a noun but an adjective describing "Something, Someone, more beautiful still." When he followed the highest and the best in his transcendent experiences, they led him to God.

V.   One of the things that most powerfully tempts me to be a Christian, and that most firmly keeps me a Christian, *is my sense of responsibility to others.*

It is easy to be careless about ourselves and about our own commitment to faith. And then we fall in love. We meet someone who becomes more precious to us than our own life, and we begin to shape our future together. But what kind of life is it going to be? What values will it cherish? Will our home be a Christian home? And then we know that if our life together does not hold in itself the richness of Christian faith it will be poor indeed.

Or we bring a wee baby into the world, and it is so precious to us that we can hardly bear it. My own daughter, Heather, speaking of her own little two-year-old, said to me the other day, "Sometimes I love her so much I can hardly bear it." You have little ones and you love them so much you can hardly stand it. Your own life matters nothing to you when you compare it with the value of theirs, for you would gladly die for them. But what quality of life will be theirs? What values will you teach them, what relationship will define them? Are they going to hear the story of Jesus and His love? Are they going to be brought up in a Christian home? Let one generation allow the faith to fall, you see, and it is lost. If not for our own sake, then for theirs, we feel the tug of faith.

Let me ask you: If you were to give yourself to Him today in a new and deeper way, would you be diminished or would you be enlarged? Would your life be enriched or would it be impoverished? Would you have laid hold on the very best that is in you or the worst? There is only one answer, and that answer constitutes the temptation to be Christian.

May I say to you that this is one temptation of which it may safely be said that the best way to be rid of it is to yield to it?

TRUE SIMPLICITY

There is a great phrase in II Corinthians 11:3 — "The simplicity that is in Christ."

It is Christ's simplicity that defines yours and mine. He possesses it; we long for it. Chesterton tells us that while we rush to complexity, we yearn for simplicity. Why do we yearn for it? Because, for one thing, complexity threatens to overwhelm us. There is just too much going on; we can't cope with it. And so much that threatens the peace of our days and the tranquility of our nights seems superficial. We wish to be rid of it and long for a life that is deeper, more real and more satisfying. We find ourselves nostalgic for a simpler age, wishing that we had been born in an earlier, less bewildering time. Every age seems to us to have been more serene than our own. Or we long for a simpler religion, for the old morality that seemed to be less ambiguous and bewildering than the new.

Events seem somehow beyond our control. Helpless to deal with the great things, we manage the little things. We make gestures towards simplicity. Last week, for example, I tidied my desk and felt better for doing so. Now I have three piles of paper instead of four. Or we learn a new technique to help us organize our days. Not long ago, one of my colleagues announced that one should always do one of three things with every bit of correspondence: answer it at once, or file it, or throw it out. I have been doing that since he talked to me. I am now master of my fate and captain of my soul. What a breakthrough!

Some go even farther. I have some wealthy friends who had houses everywhere and cars everywhere and boats everywhere until they grew weary of it all and sold the lot. Well, almost. Now they have one house and two cars. They "simplified" their life.

But we know that's not it. That's a gesture, a preliminary skirmish, the easy part. These pitiful actions are but an expression of our bewilderment and helplessness; they still leave us at the edges when we know we have to travel to the center. Simplicity is more than tidying up, and no re-arrangement yields serenity. We make these gestures because we don't know what else to do. And because we don't we begin to make mistakes. Instead of finding simplicity, we become simplistic. We seek clarity by reduction. We rob things of their mystery and imagine we have solved them. Or we simplify indiscriminately. We all know people who thought to simplify their life by giving something up only to discover that they had given up the wrong thing, for they did not know the things that belonged to their peace. We don't know what to surrender, and, lacking a wise discrimination, may throw out the good with the bad. I know one man who, not knowing what to give up to simplify his life, gave up everything only to find himself staring at empty days he must somehow usefully fill.

Other friends have sought to simplify their lives by finding something new. The old diversions no longer amused, the old pursuits no longer satisfied, but a new hobby might, and a new interest can always be contrived. They ended up with one more ball to keep in the air as they juggled their way through their days.

Wise ones then begin to realize that true simplicity is not a matter of arrangement, merely, or a technique that any good business school might teach; it is not giving up this or taking up that. It is a spiritual quality. It is not to be found by going after it *by itself*, for it is one among a cluster of qualities each of which makes the others possible, and all of which run deep enough to touch the nerve of our being. Simplicity is a matter of character. It has to do with values — who we are and why we were made. We don't simplify our lives by tidying our desk or giving up tennis, but by discovering some saving priority to which we can give our whole heart. If it is to be found it will be found within us, not outside us.

One of my best friends built houses for years and then, weary of that, began to build boats. He has a theory about how and what people build, born of his knowledge of himself and his experience of others. "People build what they are," he tells me. I thought of that when I looked at some Shaker furniture the other day. It was utterly simple and beautiful in its simplicity. Shaker furniture is the expression of Shaker character. That is why the Shaker song, "Simple Gifts" is printed at the end of this chapter.

Simplicity, then, is not so much a matter of technique as it is an expression of our inner life and our spiritual depth. Dag Hammarskjold, who needed no instruction from anyone about the complexity of our world, believed that simplicity might be his as a work of grace in his soul. And so he prayed, "If only I could grow; firmer, simpler, calmer, warmer." We remember our text, "the simplicity that is in Christ," and learn from it that it is a divine vocation, not a method that might be learned at a management seminar. So if I exhort you, as I instruct myself, to a greater simplicity, what are the qualities it requires of us?

I.   *True simplicity is born of integrity.*

Integrity means being *all-of-a-piece*, where impulse of the heart, the thought of the mind, word of the mouth and action of the hand are all one simple, single expression of the whole person. That is integrity. But notice that the word the King James Version translates "simplicity," the New English Bible translates "single-heartedness," or, if you like, "single-mindedness." To have integrity means there is no contradiction in us, no "torn to piecesness" as William James described our divided self.

If we had that kind of integrity, wouldn't our life be simpler? If our view were single, if we saw clearly and did what we perceived, wouldn't that simplify our life with a deep, enduring quality? Now we begin to get a hint of something important. The opposite of simplicity is not complexity. The opposite of simplicity is insincerity, dissimulation, contradiction. If you like, lies!

Have you noticed how simple and natural the truth is? When you speak it, you don't have to remember what you said. You have just to tell it. It comes naturally, again and again. But if truth is natural, lies are unnatural. For one thing, you have to remember them. Don't be a liar if you don't have a good memory, for you're going to need it. "O what a tangled web we weave when first we practice to deceive!" One falsehood falsifies the whole world. It means we have to stop and think and work things out before we dare say anything. Having lied, the truth might give us away. Suddenly our life is infinitely more complicated than it was.

But it is worse even than that, for we can't keep the lie outside us. It invades our life and becomes part of our awareness of ourselves and the double look we have to give everything. Our openness, directness and simplicity are lost. We become false people living in a world we have made false, and that becomes very complicated indeed. No wonder it exhausts us!

> There was a crooked man who walked a crooked mile.
> He found a crooked sixpence upon a crooked style.
> He bought a crooked cat which caught a crooked mouse,
> And they all lived together in a little crooked house.

Why was everything crooked? Because the man was crooked. He was a crook. If we wish to simplify our life, the place to begin is with our own integrity.

What a difference that can make to our relationships! George MacDonald, speaking of one of the deepest relationships of life, asks, "What is our first duty to each other?" And his answer is, "To be what we appear." Simple, isn't it? And profound! If we were to allow our integrity to pervade our relationships, if we were to people what we appear, what a welcome relief it would bring from our carefully projected image, our pretence, our hypocrisy. Not only would our life be saved from dissimulation, it would gain enormously in style. Says George Orwell, speaking of literature, "Nothing helps a good style like sincerity." If you know what it is you want to say, and wish to be understood when you say it, your words will be short, clear, precise and readily received. They will have what William Blake, poet and engraver, called "the hard line of rectitude" about them. But if you're not sure what you want to say, or if, being sure, you want to deceive rather than reveal, your words will multiply and swell like balloons. They will confuse and not clarify; they will be long and ambiguous and will carry ten meanings, not one.

Do you ever wonder why, when our politicians make speeches, we have to have a panel of experts to tell us what they meant? Don't you think we would understand what they meant if they wanted us to? Do you know why Jesus was divine? At least part of the answer is that God was able to speak through Him a clear, revealing word. There was no division in Him. He was like the robe that He wore, woven in one piece, without seam. He had what the New Testament calls "purity of heart." There was no contradiction in Him. What He felt, He thought; and what He thought, He said; and what He said, He did. When you saw Him you saw all of Him. When you heard Him you had the truth of Him. And when He looked at you He was fully present to you. And through this wholeness God's word came clearly.

II.   *True simplicity is kin to humility.*

François Fenelon, the French Archbishop who made profound things so simple so often, said, "Simplicity is the uprightness of the soul that is not absorbed with itself. It is the quality that belongs to those who have made a perfect renunciation of themselves."

When I read that definition of simplicity, it reminded me immediately of Dag Hammarskjold's definition of humility. He said, "Humility is to perceive reality not in relation to ourselves, but in its sacred independence. It is to see it from that point of rest in ourselves." Notice that they are both saying the same thing. One is talking about simplicity, the other about humility, and they're both saying that you can't have one without the other. Both simplicity and humility begin in that point of rest in ourselves from which we perceive reality not in relation to ourselves, and we can't have either quality so long as we put ourselves at the center and try to make everything revolve around us.

Now, we know that. Part of the complexity of our life is that we want to do things for other people. Moved by a generous impulse, we attempt to do so but instead end up serving ourselves. We want to work for their good, but our own interests get in the way. There are times when we see clearly that the whole purpose of our life, the satisfaction of all our yearning, is to find someone to whom we can give ourselves completely, with nothing held back, so that we can say to them in all honesty, "You have all of me." It is not simply that we long for integrity, for wholeness, but that, having found it, we long to give ourselves away, unspoiled by the intrusion of our own desires, interests and appetites.

What pure pleasure it would be to know a beautiful woman and to enjoy her without wanting to possess her! Or to say with Edna St. Vincent Millay:

> I will be the gladdest thing
> Under the sun!
> I will touch a hundred flowers
> And not pick one.

That is to perceive things in their sacred independence. It is to have Hammarskjold's humility. And it is to have Fenelon's simplicity, the uprightness of a soul that is not absorbed in itself, the grace that can see and admire without needing to possess.

Have you ever thought what a genuine humility would do for our painful self-consciousness? You know how awkward we feel when we walk into a room thinking all the time that everyone is looking at us and wondering all the time what they're thinking of us. We wonder what we should say or do to end our unease. Should we try to impress them or just act naturally? But we don't know what "naturally" means. It doesn't help much even to tell ourselves that we're probably wrong in our assumption that we are the center of interest and attention. People are usually giving us much less attention than we think they are, being far more interested in themselves than they are in us. But this does not help our awkwardness. How wonderful it would be to walk into a room and be genuinely more interested in the people who are there than in the impression we were making on them! What a release to be delivered in this way from our self-consciousness! It would bring enormous freedom and lightsomeness of spirit if we could enjoy people without getting in our own way. And it would simplify our life, for all our energy, interest and attention would flow in one direction.

Or think how a genuine humility would end our competitiveness. Wouldn't it be a happy thing to be able to say of someone, "He is very good" without wondering if he is as good as we are, or whether he is so good as to threaten us? Wouldn't it elevate us if we could be glad that another is so gifted without wondering if his gifts are greater than our own? What serenity and peace such a humility would bring, and how it would simplify our life to be rid of the competitiveness that adds tension to our days. Says St. Thomas à Kempis, "The humble in spirit dwell in a multitude of peace." The humble in spirit, not the inordinately competitive in spirit.

Or think how a humility of this sort would release us from the strain of sustaining our image. To conceal the emptiness within, we hide behind an academic hood, or a clerical collar, or a title, or position, pretending to know more or to be better than we are. How important that we should convince others of our stature, for they in turn will help us to believe it. But the strain of it! The energy it takes! And we never do succeed in overcoming our sense of emptiness and falseness.

We are often told nowdays that we lack a sense of sin. I don't know if that's true. But let me ask whether or not you grow weary and dissatisfied with the sense of your own phoniness? What an unending effort it takes to keep up appearances and put on a front! And how empty we feel when, as Kierkegaard tells us, the midnight hour strikes when all masks come off. Who are we then, and how do we think of ourselves? And the sad thing is that we spend all that energy preserving an image when we could be delivered from our inordinate self-concern and begin to enjoy the world in its sacred independence.

In 1956 I read a sentence I have never forgotten. Written by Walter Kaufman, it contains a philosophy of life in its few words: "Only the great philosophers laugh." They laugh because they are great. They are not threatened, as little philosophers are, when their system of thought is attacked. They are secure in their ability to refine it, or to think up another one. They manage to see their search for truth and meaning as a thing in itself, not as something that has value only because it is *theirs*. And so they have a lightsome spirit. Being great, they laugh. They are at peace with themselves. They are not fretful about their own place or importance. Did you ever think that simplicity arises from a humility of this sort; from being able to perceive reality not in relation to ourselves? When we are able to do so, we see and enjoy things in their sacred independence. We are at peace with ourselves.

III.   *Simplicity is the fruit of sanctity.*

Austin Farrer, to whom I owe as much as I owe any man, said once that "sanctity is just utter simplicity before the Divine will." Does that sound difficult? It is made easy for us if we see it in the life of Christ. It means that Jesus moved from task to task saying, "This is what God my Father wants me to do now." He came, He tells us, not to do His own will but the will of His Father who sent Him. The simplicity in Christ consisted in this, that He discovered God's will for His life, and did it. His was the simplicity of loving obedience.

Such goodness would simplify our life enormously. For one thing, it would give us our sense of priority. What a comfort to know that in any moment we are doing what we ought to be doing. Always there are a dozen conflicting claims on our time and attention and twenty useful things that we might do. But normally there is only one thing that we *must* do. To discover what it is, and to do it, is the secret not only of sanctity but simplicity.

Often we complicate our lives because, while we want to

put first things first, we don't know which things *are* first
things. So we blunder from task to task with no saving priority
to guide us. We have impetus but no direction and end up by
doing a bit of this and a bit of that. We are like Stephen
Leacock's celebrated Lord Ronald who "flung himself from
the room, flung himself upon his horse and rode madly off in
all directions."

This is of great practical importance to me, for it would be
impossible to be minister of this great church without having a
clear sense of priorities. My priorities have been chosen and
will be adhered to. I want to love you as much as I can and
preach to you as well as I can. Those two things have first
claim on my time and attention. Of the many things I might
do, perhaps even of the many things I ought to do, these will be
done first.

The choosing of one's priorities brings a sense of peace. An
awareness of what one is called to do makes the big decision
for us, and making the big decision makes many of the little
ones. If I am a Christian, for example, I don't have to discover
a new set of values every day. Being a Christian is enough to
decide many questions of behavior and morality. What is left
for me is not to discover new answers but to be obedient and
faithful to the truth I already know. Someone once asked
Willie Mays the secret of his success as a baseball player. He
replied, "When they throw it, I hit it, and when they hit it, I
catch it." Massively simple, but those fundamentals contain all
the subtleties of the greatest game in the world. The fundamentals are clear, the refinement is inexhaustible.

I see this clearly in the life and work of Mother Teresa. She
moves from task to task with an enormous serenity while the
rest of us, with far fewer demands upon our time and thought,
live our lives of quiet desperation. And she does so, not
because she is very clever, but because she is good. She knows
what Jesus wants her to do for love of Him, and she does it.
And she does it with grace and humor. Because it is for Him,
she does it as beautifully as she can. She does something beautiful for God.

What does God want you to do? To begin with, He wants

you to pray. And it pleases Him when you do your work well
and care for those entrusted to your love. He longs for truth in
your inward parts, and that you should praise what is worthy
of honor. Start there, and see not only what simplicity, but
what richness, your life will have.

'Tis the gift to be simple
'Tis the gift to be free
'Tis the gift to come down where you ought to be.
And when we find ourselves in the place just right
'Twill be the valley of love and delight.

When true simplicity is gained,
To bow and to bend we shan't be ashamed.
To turn, turn, will be our delight
'Till by turning, turning, we come round right.

A Shaker Poem. c 1840

THE MOVING FINGER

I have a quotation for you from Meister Eckhart, a thirteenth century mystic and one of the greatest preachers of his age. Most of the time he was in trouble with his Archbishop who accused him of heresy. Eckhart appealed to the Pope, was summoned to Rome for a hearing, but died before any verdict was delivered. He said: "Only the hand that erases can write the true thing." Write that on the back of your mind and allow it to comfort and hearten you for the rest of your life.

William Walton knew a good story when he heard one, and when he read the account of Belshazzar's Feast in the Book of Daniel he knew he had to set it to music, and he did. He set it to music that will send a shudder through you, as the story itself will. Belshazzar, King of Babylon, threw a great party and used in the orgy the holy vessels pillaged from the Temple in Jerusalem. Imagine! The harlots and concubines of Babylon entertained themselves with the sacred vessels of Israel! It was a repeat of an old story, for Belshazzar was overreaching himself as his father Nebuchadnezzar had done.

Suddenly the revellers discovered that the banquet was haunted. A mysterious hand appeared and wrote a cryptic message on the wall. What did the writing mean? Nobody at the feast knew, so they sent for Daniel, and Daniel, the man of God, interpreted it: "Your kingdom is at an end. Your life will be taken. Your power is over. Your dominion will be divided and given to others." "That very night," says the Word, "Belshazzar king of Babylon died, and the kingdom was given to Darius the Mede."

What did the hand write? It wrote, "Thou hast been weighed in the balance and found wanting!" So clear! So simple! So final! So absolute!

> The Moving Finger writes; and, having writ,
> Moves on: nor all thy Piety nor Wit
> Shall lure it back to cancel half a Line,
> Nor all thy Tears wash out a Word of it.

What if those words were written of you or me? "Thou hast been weighed in the balance and found wanting!" They are true, aren't they? How could we resist the truth of them? We don't need anyone to tell us that we are lightweights; that we have less stuff in us than we ought to have; that there is less to us than there might be. And then there comes the word of Eckhart, so full of hope and grace; not speaking of the finger that writes and having writ moves on so that we can never call it back, but of the hand that erases in order to write the true thing. The most important thing about us is not what has been written, but that what has been written may be rubbed out, erased by the need to write a deeper truth.

Why is it that only the hand that erases can write the true thing? There are several reasons.

I.   *Only the hand that erases can write the true thing because our knowledge is partial.*

It is necessary because, as the Apostle Paul tells us, "we know only in part." If we could see truth, see it clearly and see it whole, then maybe we wouldn't have to rub out things in order to write the true thing. But that is not the human condition. Rather, "we see but the baffling reflections in a mirror." Plato confirms the Apostle's insight. He tells us that all our knowledge is like shadows cast on the wall of a cave by a flickering firelight outside. It is because our knowledge is fragmentary that we have to rub it out and write it again, only better.

One of my old professors at McMaster University was a scientist in the Department of Biology. He told me once that the department brought a distinguished biologist to the university to deliver a public lecture. The man's plane was delayed by fog, and the audience was kept waiting. Finally he arrived, very late and very apologetic. Seeking to reassure him,

the chairman of the evening said that the visitor was so distinguished that the audience would have been willing to wait any
length of time for the opportunity to hear him. Then the
scientist replied, "But you do not understand! Do you not realize that in the time you waited someone could have made a
discovery that would make everything I say to you obsolete?"

Such is the pace of scientific discovery that we must be prepared constantly to erase what we think we know in order to
write the true thing. We used to think that the earth was the
center of the universe and that the sun circled it. Rub that out
and write the true thing! We used to think that the world was
flat. Seafarers were afraid to lose sight of land for fear of
dropping over the edge. Rub that out and write the true thing!
You can sail straight on and circle the globe!

The same is true of medicine. We easily forget the superstition that once surrounded the practice of medicine. We are
told that when Charles II of England was ill, a pint of blood
was taken from the royal right arm and a half-pint from the
royal left shoulder. His head was shaved and a blister raised.
Then sneezing powder was given to him, and then a plaster of
pitch, and then forty drops of abstract of human skull, and
then, we are told, the king gave up the ghost. You could hardly
blame him. Nowdays, we wouldn't take blood out, we'd put it
in. Rub that out and write the true thing!

I have a friend who is a distinguished radiologist. He is a
relatively young man, even younger than I am. He told me not
long ago that about eighty percent of what he does every day
has little to do with what he was taught in university. Most of
what he was taught in medical school is gone for ever. Rub
that out and write the true thing!

Something of the sort is true of philosophy. Descartes
longed to make a new philosophy based on certain knowledge
rather than on mere speculation. How was he to find certainty?
By erasing all that had been taught and written and by beginning with one thing he was absolutely sure of. What could he
be absolutely sure of? The one thing he could not doubt was
that he was at that moment thinking. And so we have his
famous *Cogito Ergo Sum*, "I think, therefore I am." Descartes

did not succeed in his enterprise, but he altered our perception of reality for ever. And I can quote others, ranging all the way from the Buddha to Thomas Hardy, who say the same thing. Don't believe things just because others have thought them; believe them because you can discover with your own thought what is true. Rub that out and write the true thing!

Perhaps you think I am making heavy weather of this, and that the point has been well enough taken. But have you taken it deeply enough into yourself that you apply it to your faith? Some people become angry with anyone or anything that disturbs their thinking, yet they haven't had a refreshing thought about their religion for half a lifetime. Questions distress them, doubts depress them. They seem not to realize that it is by questions and doubts that we learn to erase what is written that we may write the true thing. That is why one of the greatest of poets exhorts us to be patient towards all that is unsolved in our hearts and learn to love the questions themselves. Do you manage to do it? I wish for you progress and joy in the faith, but you won't have either if you're not willing to erase what is written that you may write what is true.

The first charge ever brought against Christians was atheism. Once they believed in the God and Father of our Lord Jesus Christ, all other conceptions of God had to go. Now "the true thing" was the One who was the Way, the Truth and the Life, and all other ideas of God were judged by Him. We have ideas about God that are less than Christian, that are unworthy of the revelation we have in Christ. We need to rub those ideas out and write the Word that is full of grace and truth.

II.   *Only the hand that erases can write the true thing because our lives are imperfect.*

I wish you could have met my friend Harry Moore whom I knew fifteen years ago. He was a scout for the greatest team in baseball which is, as we all know, The Detroit Tigers. Harry was not only a scout for the Tigers, he wrote poetry as well. He loved to talk about baseball, and his Christian faith, and his verses. Most of what he wrote was not very good. Harry knew it, but it didn't bother him. He wrote his poetry, not to show it to anyone, but because it satisfied a deep need in him, as the poetry we secretly write satisfies a deep need in us. All over the church are people who write poetry. Most of them are wise or kind enough not to show it to anyone. They write it because they have poetry in them and it is the poetry, not the prose, that is the deepest truth of them. Now and then Harry Moore would come up with a line decent enough to last a while. Take this one, for example:

> I wish I had the time
> gone by;
> I'd use it differently
> than I
> Have done.
> But then, 'tis likely
> soon I'd find
> I'd made mistakes
> of another kind.

Whatever you think of Harry's poetry, it is hard to resist Harry's truth.

Says Schweitzer, "If only we were fourteen again!" We think we wouldn't make any mistakes if we were fourteen again. Well, not the same ones, anyway. Harry was right. We'd make mistakes of another kind. Do you know why? Because imperfection is part of our life and part of our world. That's what the doctrine of Original Sin really means; that the ambiguity, the imperfection is not incidental, passing, marginal. It is characteristic, fundamental, defining. But if this is so, then we must realize that we live by grace, not by justice, and it is grace that erases that it may write the true thing.

There is an old story of a woman who was having her portrait painted and who encouraged the young artist with the exhortation that he should try to do her justice. The painter was not wise, and he was not gallant; but he had a love of truth and so he replied, "Madam, what you need is not justice but mercy." Justice isn't enough, and the reason is plain: Justice by itself is less than just. Justice without mercy ceases even to be justice. Only the hand that erases can write the true thing. If you are not willing to forgive me, you will never know me. Forgiveness is the condition of knowledge. Mercy is the condition of insight. That is why we praise justice but hate the just man. Says one character, "You have no tenderness, only justice, and therefore you are unjust." Do you live by justice? No friendship, no marriage, not even your own self-respect can exist merely on justice. We live by mercy.

I was thinking the other day of an incident I read years ago. I believe it was in A. J. Cronin's autobiography. He describes being a physician in the North of England when there was an outbreak of diphtheria. A little boy was brought in hardly able to breathe. As the Irish would say, "he had the dip," and in those days that often meant that the patient would die. The doctor performed a tracheotomy which allowed the child to breathe, and put him in the care of a young nurse who would watch him through the night hours. The doctor went off to bed for a much-needed rest.

In the small hours of the morning, a trembling nurse wakened him with the news that the little boy was dead. Exhausted herself, the nurse had slipped into sleep only to awaken and discover that the tube was blocked and the child dead. The physician was furious. He raged against the girl. He told her he would make sure she would never nurse again. She stood before his wrath pitifully thin, undernourished, devasted by what had happened, and in a pathetic voice scarcely audible said, "Give me another chance!" He told her he would not, and having dismissed her, went back to bed.

Back to bed, but not to sleep. Her poor face haunted him, and so did her words, "give me another chance!" The next morning, when he got up, he tore up the letter of condemnation he had written the night before. Years later, Cronin tells us, he met the young girl, now grown to womanhood, the Matron of one of the greatest children's hospitals in England and renowned throughout the country for her commitment to her calling and her skill in caring for little ones who were ill. "Give me another chance!" she had asked, and he had done it.

"Only the hand that erases can write the true thing."

We dismiss people too easily. We identify them with their sin. We judge them by what they do, not by what they intend. We allow them no excuse. But that is not how we deal with ourselves. We do not identify ourselves with our sin, we separate ourselves from it. We do not say, "I am a fool!" We say, "I did a foolish thing." We judge our intention, not our action. What we did had a serious outcome, but we *meant* well, and so we excuse ourselves. We do that readily for ourselves, but reluctantly, if at all, for others.

Charles Morgan once wrote an appeal for kindness: "I said a foolish thing, I wish I could unsay it. But you alone can unsay it by not remembering my foolishness when you remember me." Do you know why we find it so hard to believe that we are forgiven? It is because we are so reluctant to forgive. We remember for ourselves, but forget for others, that it is only the hand that erases that can write the true thing. To know the truth of this is to move beyond justice to mercy.

III. *Only the hand that erases can write the true thing, because our creation is unfinished.*

Our creation unfinished? Do we not say that "in the beginning the Lord God created . . ."? Is that not a completed work? Some of us think it is. It all happened away back in inaccessible time or far out there in unreachable space.

Well, I can't make any kind of sense of a creation that is past, for the truth of us is not that we were created but that we are being created. The only doctrine of creation that is any good is one that affirms that creation is now.

For example, you will not be the same person going out of this church this morning that you were when you came into it. You may not be greatly changed, but you will certainly be different. Sometimes people have come in and their whole life has been transformed. And now we begin to see that it is impossible to speak of creation without speaking of re-creation. It is not only that we have been created, but that we are being re-created all the time. We not only change, we hope to improve! There are habits we hope to give up, music we have yet to hear, people we have yet to meet. All this reminds us that we are not yet complete. God did not wind up a universe and leave it to tick its way to the finish. He has ends, purposes, goals for His world and for us, and that means that He is all the time present by His creative Spirit shaping and reshaping us. The very words spoken in this instant of time will change you and me by the speaking and the hearing of them! That is why the hand must erase to write the true thing. We are novel creatures, full of surprises, changing all the time, leaving an old self behind and finding a new self to be.

I recently spoke to Dr. Jones, our Associate Minister, when he was trying to tidy up a few things up before leaving for a few days. He had no business being about the place at all, and I told him to be off. He didn't pay any attention to me at all. But later he said, "When I get to heaven, I'm going to tell God that I am terribly sorry, but there were a great many things I didn't have time to finish." And I replied, "Ken, *if* you get to heaven God will say, 'Dr. Jones, don't worry about those unfinished things because I haven't finished with you yet.' "

And he hasn't finished with you yet! There are many things in your life whose significance is not yet decided. What their meaning will be nobody knows, not even you. What we do know is that out of all the stuff of our life, God will bring forth a unique good. Out of *all* the stuff of our life, not just the good bits. Get rid of the idea of "good bits" for ever. There are no good bits. There is just you, and you are a mixture. Your good bits are touched by evil and your bad bits are touched by good; and it is the work of God's grace to do something with this strange mixture that we are. Perfect wisdom and unwearied love have an inexhaustible power to draw out of it a new and better thing.

I was with Malcolm Muggeridge at his home in Sussex when the telephone rang and Collins, his publisher, informed him that they were going to publish his diaries. Malcolm was elated. And then he said, "You know, the temptation is to clean them up." He went on, "But I can't do that, because if I did it would not be *me*. If the story is to have any value it must be about me as I am and was, not as I ought to have been or might have been."

You are not perfect, and neither am I, but out of all our imperfections God is making a great good, unique and unrepeatable. Nobody else in the whole world is like you, and He is shaping and re-shaping you out of that strange confusion of good and bad that you have offered Him. "Only the hand that erases can write the true thing."

Do you remember the beginning of the movie, "Lawrence of Arabia"? Lawrence snuffs out a match with his bare fingers and says, "Nothing is written!" and so affirms his freedom and the openness of the future. While much is written there is a hand that erases. And it is poised to write the true thing.

WHAT EASTER GIVES BACK TO US

St. John 20:1-17

"Jesus said, 'Mary!' She turned to Him and said, 'My Master!' "

On this Easter morning I want to talk to you about what someone has called the greatest recognition scene in all literature: that between Mary Magdalene and Jesus in the Garden of the Resurrection.

Nobody loved Jesus more than Mary did. He knew her love for Him. He said that having been forgiven much, she loved much. She had good reason to love Him because He had loved her into a higher life. She is described as "a woman who was living an immoral life." But that seldom is the whole story about people. Immoral though we are, we still have longings and aspirations after goodness and beauty. One day her hunger led her to His feet where she saw all that her true self longed for. She washed His feet with her tears and wiped them with the hairs of her head; and when she had done so, she heard from His lips words that meant her life would never be the same again, "Thy faith hath saved thee; go in peace."

Kahil Gibran has Jesus speaking to Mary, "You have many lovers, but I alone love you. Other men have loved themselves in your nearness, I love you in yourself. Other men see a beauty in you that shall fade sooner than their own years. I see a beauty in you that shall not fade away, and in the autumn of your days that beauty shall not be afraid to gaze at itself in the mirror and it shall not be offended. I alone love the unseen in you." And Mary adds, "On that day the sunset of His eyes slew the dragon in me and I became a woman."

How many loved your moments of glad grace,
And loved your beauty with love false or true,
But one man loved the pilgrim soul in you,
And loved the sorrows of your changing face.

No wonder she loved Him! And then on Good Friday it seemed it was all over. She could have said on Good Friday what she said on Easter Sunday, "They have taken away my Lord." The Master whom she loved, who was her life, was crucified, and her world became a Good Friday world. All that she loved she had lost. And then, early on Easter day, in the mists of morning she looked into His sepulchre and found it empty. Numbed by grief and half blinded by tears, she caught a glimpse of Him but mistook Him for the gardener. Her anguished words asked Him to tell her, if he had taken away her Lord, where he had laid Him. And then Jesus said, "Mary!"

What's in a name? A whole world of life and beauty is in a name when it is spoken like that. No one ever spoke her name as He spoke it, and suddenly she moved to the other side of darkness, from a Good Friday world into an Easter world, from evening to morning, and everything she had lost was given back to her.

Easter gives back to us everything that Good Friday takes from us. It is Jesus Himself, and in having Him restored to us we move from the night of dereliction to the morning of God's laughter. But what does it mean to say that on Easter morning He is given back to us?

I.   *He gives Himself back to us and in so doing He gives us eternal life.*

Indeed, He not only gives us eternal life, He declares its nature to be a loving relationship with Himself. Jesus spoke her name, "Mary!" and she said, "My Master!" With those words, the love they had for each other was fresh and new again but with this difference: it was now a love that had passed through death undiminished. It was the love of Christ reaching her from the other side of death, and what is that but eternal life? In speaking her name He declared to Mary what He declares to each of us, that He is ours forever, that He holds us to Himself so closely that not even death can part us. And that is to declare that eternal life is a loving relationship with Himself.

As soon as we forget this, eternal life loses its quality. It becomes nothing more than endless life, a quantity of time rather than a quality of relationship. Indeed, it loses any quality that would make it desirable. Who would wish for mere endlessness without quality? It would be something to escape from, not something to be coveted.

H. L. Mencken once declared with characteristic frankness that endless life was nothing more than sheer egotism going on for ever and ever. He asserted that he neither believed it nor wanted it. Huxley pointed out with irresistible candor that many of those who desire immortal life are at a loss to know what to do with themselves on a wet Sunday afternoon. One of our poets suggests that endless life might be like waiting for ever in a railway station for a train that never comes. Woody Allen, one of my favorite theologians, thinks that it might be having to listen to Howard Cosell forever! When there is no quality, eternal life is not worth having, and what gives it its quality is a loving relationship.

We prove this in small ways. How long is an hour? Well, it all depends who you're with, doesn't it? Eternal life is not endlessness. Eternal life is a loving relationship with Jesus Christ, and it is the quality of His friendship that defines its nature.

Again, when we forget that eternal life is a loving relationship with Christ, the value of the individual is easily lost. Some religions teach that when we die, the self is not lost but becomes part of a larger whole, rather like a drop of water dropping into a pail of water. The self is still there, but can no longer be separated and recognized as an individual self. But to be no longer a center of self-awareness, to lose the sense of oneself as a heart of love that can be linked in love with other hearts, is to have less there than we have here. It is to envision an eternal life in which we have less personal reality and poorer personal relationships than we enjoy now.

When we lose our self-awareness, and our awareness of others, we have lost ourselves and them. Dylan Thomas failed to see this. He wrote a magnificent poem called "And Death Shall Have No Dominion." In it, he declares that death shall have no dominion because, "while lovers be lost love shall not." It sounds not only defiant, but triumphant. Then we remember that if lovers be lost, death has dominion enough, for there is no love when all lovers perish. How can love *not* be lost if Tom is lost who loves Mary,and if Margaret is lost who loves George? If Jack loses his Jill there is no comfort in telling him that death has no dominion. Losing his dear love, he has lost everything! Caitlin, the wife of Dylan Thomas, affirmed the truth of this after her husband's death in New York City. She wrote a book and called it *Leftover Life To Kill*. When she lost her Dylan, death had proved its dominion.

If we declare the nature of eternal life by saying it is a loving relationship with Jesus Christ, then we are saying it is not something that begins when we die but a quality of life we may have here and now. All the leaves of the New Testament are rustling with this news. Eternal life is ours already if we know and love Christ. The love that claims us from the other side of death by speaking our name is the love that invites us to His friendship *now*. Having Him, we have eternal life.

One of the men who most influenced Henry Emerson Fosdick of Riverside Church was a Quaker theologian and philosopher called Rufus Jones. Years ago he went to England to preach and lecture. While he was in England his son in America died. There were no jet planes then to thrust him back to North America in a few hours. Rufus Jones could not get home for his son's funeral. On the day of the funeral his friends in England marvelled at his grace and serenity, and told him so. He replied that the secret of his calm was massively simple. All their life his son and he had loved and been loved by Jesus Christ. The Christian hope of Rufus Jones for his son was the conviction that "where there is so much love there must be more."

That is what Mary discovered. Christian hope is the love of God. It affirms that where there is so much love, there must be more. The love of Christ will not allow even death to separate us from Him. P. T. Forsyth, one of the greatest of theologians, tells us that eternal life is very simple: What it means is that there is a life with Jesus here, and there is a life with Jesus there. That is the quality of it and that is why we want it. He gives us Himself, and not only gives us eternal life but declares the nature of it.

II. *He gave Himself back to them, and in giving them Himself He gave them themselves.*

It wasn't simply that Easter gave Jesus back to the disciples. They discovered that having Him meant they had recovered their own selves.

Jesus had defined them. He had not only called them, He had given them a calling. They were His disciples, discovering who they were by their relationship with Him. He had kindled their faith. He had made them fishers of men, had sent them forth in His name and given them a Gospel to preach. And then, suddenly, this Man who held their life's meaning in his own Being was taken away from them, and that was the end. It wasn't simply that they had lost Him, it was that in losing Him they had lost themselves. In a profound sense, the best that was in them died when He was crucified, and they no longer knew who they were, for they had known themselves only in Him.

A newspaper editor in England once asked his daughter who worked for him to write an article about David Livingstone, the Christian medical missionary to Africa. The editor had no sympathy with David Livingstone's faith, so he told his daughter to write the article without mentioning it. She went off to do all the research necessary for the article, but soon returned to tell her father that what he had asked her to do was impossible. She said that her article would not only mention Livingstone's religion, but would make it its major interest, for David Livingstone could not be explained apart from his faith. It defined him, making him what he was and giving him his life's work. What he did, he did for love of Christ.

All Christians would wish to make a similar claim. For all our failure to be like Him, we are still inexplicable apart from Him. Any good that is in us, any depth we possess, we owe to Him. Anything that is lovely, or true, or gracious in us has come to us from His grace by His graciousness. Without Him I do not know who I am or what I ought to be. He has shaped my attitudes from within. He tells me who I am.

Some of us may feel like resisting the truth of this, for it seems that if we affirm it we have handed ourselves away, defining ourselves in terms of someone else. Yet something of the same is true of our friends and dear ones. Our friends make us what we are, each one winning from us a unique response and bringing us alive in his or her own unique way. I am never exactly the same in my response to any two friends, not because my personality is unstable, but because each person I love calls to life a different part of me. That is what we mean when we talk about the uniqueness of human personality. Each unique person wins from us a unique response. That is why we cannot talk lightly about personal uniqueness, because when we lose that unique person, it is not simply that they die, it is that the bit of us they brought alive perishes with them. When we weep for our beloved dead, we weep not only for them, but for ourselves. That is why John Donne exhorts us not to ask for whom the funeral bell tolls; it tolls for us. Each person's death diminishes me, for the part of me they made alive dies with them.

If you have lost a dear one you will know the truth of this. A friend of mine in my London church once talked to me about her husband who had died, and whom I had buried. She said, "He gave me my place." And knowing him, I know he would have been eager to say the same thing of her. Our friends give us our place. Some of us may like to think that we are more independent than that, but why should we wish to be? Should we be more genuinely human if we could say that we do not need our friends? If we do not need our friends we are not more truly human, we are more poorly adjusted and more deeply impoverished. My dependence on those I love is not an expression of weakness but a self-affirming reality. I couldn't live a week without the love and trust, the acceptance and companionship of my friends.

That is how the disciples felt about Jesus, and why they were devastated by His death. He had promised them, "I will not leave you comfortless," and the word He used meant that He would not allow them to be orphaned. But it seemed that soon after He made His promise, He broke it. They *were* orphaned, they were bereft when their master was crucified. Suddenly the One who had given their life any meaning it had was gone. Now they were servants without a Master, disciples without a Teacher, evangelists without a Gospel. And then on Easter Sunday morning He fulfilled His promise by giving Himself back to them, and in so doing gave back to them their own life. Notice the difference it made to them once they knew that their beloved Master was alive. After His crucifixion they had huddled together in fear; but now, in the words of their enemies, they "turned the world upside down," which just means that they put it right way up.

That is why the evidence for our Lord's resurrection is not merely the New Testament account of it. The best evidence for the resurrection is that there *is* a New Testament, that there was a community to produce it, that there was a faith to prod-uce the community, and men and women to preach that faith. And they did so only because when Jesus gave Himself back to them, He gave them back themselves and their faith. They rediscovered their courage and went on with their Master's ministry of reconciliation. That is the second thing, and it brings us to the third and last.

III. *In giving them Himself He gave back to them their own beloved dead.*

It is Paul who puts the matter simply and clearly when he tells the Corinthians that if Christ has not been raised from the dead, then those who have fallen asleep in Him have perished. But being raised from the dead He has brought life and immortality to light through the Gospel.

When archaeologists began to examine Roman cemeteries, they found seven letters inscribed on many tombstones. They were the letters N F F N S N C. The words the letters stood for were so well known that they didn't have to be written in full; the letters were enough to declare their message. The words, of course, were Latin, and their meaning declared, "I was not, I was, I am not, I care not."

Imagine writing on a tombstone, "I care not." I can understand a person saying of himself that he didn't care whether he lived or died; I have heard people say that. There have been times and moods when most of us have felt like that. But I cannot understand anyone saying it of someone they love. Archaeologists went into the tomb of one of the Pharaohs and they found a sarcophagus containing the mummified remains of a little child and a message the child's mother had left with her little one. She had written, "O my life, my love, my little one, would God I had died for thee!" I don't care? Prince Andre in *War And Peace*, tells us that what convinces us of eternal life is not any argument; it is just that we go through life hand in hand with someone and then suddenly that someone is taken away from somewhere into nowhere, and we stand looking down into emptiness and the abyss.

But our dear ones, however deeply we love them, do not return from the abyss. Our heart breaks for their loss, but they do not come back. They have entered that country from whose bourn no traveller returns. Death gives back nothing it has taken.

When W. B. Yeats was an old man he found a bleached bone on the shore and made it speak. It said, "Death, give back to me three things. Give me the little one who found satisfaction and rest at my breast. Give me back the man who found his fulfillment in loving me, and give me back the man whom I loved and adored." But death doesn't give anything back.

Let me speak to you the saddest words, I think, in literature. They are in *King Lear*. Do you remember Lear weeping for dear Cordelia, his daughter, who is dead, and lamenting that a dog, and a horse, and a rat have life and Cordelia has no breath in her? And he weeps, "Thou'lt come no more, never, never, never, never, never!" There is a sob of heartbreak and desolation in every repeated word that tolls like a funeral bell.

When Mencken asserted that egotism is the root of our desire for eternal life, he was wrong. It is not egotism but love that demands it. It is not simply that I cannot bear that you should perish; it is that there is in you such grace, wisdom and goodness that you *ought* not to perish. If you do, then death mocks the highest and best we have loved and known by depriving us of them for ever. But when Jesus says, "Mary!" and gives Himself back to her, in that gift He gives back to us all our dear ones who have fallen asleep in Him.

About 450 years before Christ, Euripides wrote *Alcestis*. It is a play about Alcestis, a young and beautiful queen who dies willingly for her husband, the King. Heracles, the Greek Samson, comes to the king's court and learns that this dear, loving wife is dead, and that the King is broken by grief. So Heracles asks where the dark valley is that holds her, for he will go and wrestle with death to recover the woman so deeply loved by so many. And so he does. The most powerful scene in the play is that in which Heracles comes into the King's presence, accompanied by a white veiled form and addresses the King: "Look, O King, if there be aught here that seems to thee like unto thy wife, then step forth from grief to bliss." Then he removes the veil and there is Alcestis in all her radiant beauty. Heracles declares, "Here, O King, I give her back to thee."

That is just an old play, but there is another story that is nearly as old and it is much more than a play. It is the Gospel of our Lord Jesus Christ who is our Champion in the Field. It is Christ who speaks one name in a garden, and in speaking that name speaks your name and the names of those whom you have loved long since and lost awhile, and whom you have never stopped loving, and for whom you constantly pray with all the longing of your soul. And speaking their names and ours He gives them back to us, that we may step forth from grief to bliss.

I wish you could have met Mrs. Bunting. When I knew her

she was over eighty. She lived in the little seaside resort and fishing village of Donaghadee on the coast of County Down, Northern Ireland. Mrs. Bunting was old when I knew her, and she was getting ready to die. She said to me, "Mr. Boyd, I am not afraid to die because I have a claim in heaven." I asked her to tell me about it and she replied, "When I was very young I had a little baby girl, and she died when she was very small. But I have never stopped loving her. My love has followed her into the great beyond and stayed with her all through the years. I am not afraid to die because I have a claim in heaven. A little bit of myself is already there."

You have a claim in heaven, don't you? Some of those whom you love more than you love your own life are there, and they are your claim. And Jesus is there, and He is our claim. He is our claim because in His great love He has claimed us by speaking our name as once in the garden He spoke Mary's. And in speaking it, He gives us Heaven.